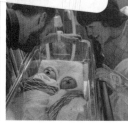

D0467306

Praise for A Coat of Yellow Paint

"*Refreshing* . . . that is a word I'd use to describe *A Coat of Yellow Paint*. Naomi's lighthearted candor about the reality of being a mama, the importance of faith, and the need for authenticity in this world will leave you nodding your head (and laughing) as you turn the pages. And she's right: all we can do is love fully, smile in response to the haters, and know that we are doing the best we can."
—GABBY BERNSTEIN, #1 *NEW YORK TIMES* BESTSELLING AUTHOR

"Naomi's storytelling is warm, inviting, and vulnerable—like you're sitting down with a new acquaintance but feel like you've been friends for years. Women from all walks of life—whether you're a mom, an entrepreneur, a twentysomething right out of college—will see something of themselves in her essays about claiming your confidence when it isn't easy, taking leaps of faith to follow your dreams, and finding the peace in figuring it all out as you go along."
—REBECCA MINKOFF, FOUNDER, REBECCA MINKOFF
AND THE FEMALE FOUNDER COLLECTIVE

"This book gives a behind-the-scenes and heartfelt look into the life of a mother, wife, and entrepreneur who created a unique job for herself by just being herself, with all the ups and downs that come with it. Through a series of stories, you discover the lessons Naomi has learned through various points of her life—from parenting to body image acceptance to handling criticism from others. Some stories are silly, some sad, some funny, and some poignant. And, they are lessons that I took away with me as I turned each and every page of this book that gives a glimpse into the roots of Naomi's inspirational story."
—JOY CHO, AUTHOR; FOUNDER AND CREATIVE DIRECTOR, OH JOY!

"Whether you feel like an old friend of Naomi's, thanks to her intimate musings as a mama of five on her wildly successful *Love Taza* blog, or are curious about how her deeply personal insights might help you create a life you love, *A Coat of Yellow Paint* is for you. Naomi's gift is the art of hearing the music through the noise, and in characteristic cheerfulness (even the sad parts will make you laugh sometimes) she deftly guides us through what it takes to make choices with purpose and find brightness on the other side of the storm, to create a life full of meaning, happiness, and plenty of reasons to use too many exclamation points!!!!!!!!!!!! Enjoy!"

—DAPHNE OZ, *NEW YORK TIMES* BESTSELLING AUTHOR AND EMMY-WINNING TV HOST

"Naomi's delightfully entertaining essays serve up a savory selection of all the feel-good life glimpses we come to her for, from her reflections on raising a young family in the magic of the big city to her colorful creativity. More meaningful though is the calming reassurance her stories give us— that through the changes and challenges of life and motherhood, the most constant thing we have to cling to is love for our families and trust in our strong inner voice, which will never fail us and will always lead us home."

—KELLE HAMPTON, *NEW YORK TIMES* BESTSELLING AUTHOR

"The daily pressures of work, family, and just being a person in the world can leave us feeling worn out and stretched thin. The essays in *A Coat of Yellow Paint* remind us to slow down, delight in small joys, and enjoy making the memories with our loved ones, especially on the days life feels like organized chaos."

—ALEXA VON TOBEL, *NEW YORK TIMES* BESTSELLING AUTHOR, FOUNDER & MANAGING PARTNER OF INSPIRED CAPITAL

"In her book, *A Coat of Yellow Paint*, Naomi shares with readers the secret of life. Through her insights we come to know that when we truly understand our own unique divine purpose and identity, life becomes joyful. Naomi not only helps us relish our experiences and see the joy and humor in them but she shows us how, through her example. I hope you will enjoy and learn from the truths she shares on her life's journey and then go paint something in your life yellow! In fact, look for the brightness of yellow paint in all your own life experiences, because it's there!"

—ELAINE S. DALTON, MOTHER, AUTHOR, AND SPEAKER

A COAT OF YELLOW PAINT

MOVING THROUGH THE NOISE TO LOVE THE LIFE YOU LIVE

Naomi Davis

HARPER
HORIZON

Published by Harper Horizon, an imprint of HarperCollins Focus LLC.

Any internet addresses, phone numbers, or company or product information printed in this book are offered as a resource and are not intended in any way to be or to imply an endorsement by Harper Horizon, nor does Harper Horizon vouch for the existence, content, or services of these sites, phone numbers, companies, or products beyond the life of this book.

Interior graphics designed by Amanda Jane Jones.

ISBN 978-0-7852-3869-0 (eBook)
ISBN 978-0-7852-3868-3 (HC)

Library of Congress Control Number: 2020942469

Printed in the United States of America
21 22 23 24 25 LSC 10 9 8 7 6 5 4 3 2 1

For you, the reader—
—and anyone who is striving to move
through the noise, like me

Contents

PART 6: YOU'VE GOT A FRIEND IN ME

PART 7: FAMILY FIRST

PART 8: FAITH IS LIKE A LITTLE SEED

PART 9: TUNE OUT THE NOISE

PART 10: PACK YOUR (DIAPER) BAGS

Foreword

I remember waking up before dawn one morning in the fall of 2013 to find Naomi putting a final coat of yellow paint and wax on what had been a brown piano. She'd worked all night in the tiny living room of our eight-hundred-square-foot New York City apartment, while quietly listening to her favorite music. I was a little in shock. She had talked about doing this for months, but I hadn't done anything to help her. I thought the wooden piano was fine in its original brown color. But as I stood there for a moment, spying on her as she brushed on a unique yellowish-green paint and hummed along to Regina Spektor, I loved how this scene exemplified so much of who she is. It wasn't that the piano needed a paint job. It's that she craved to make it bright and colorful and happy and something of her own. She worked hard to do the same to the rest of our home and in our life too—whether painting walls and rearranging furniture, or starting impromptu dance parties with our children and getting the kids to laugh in ways I couldn't.

Looking back, I realize how much she did to turn a tiny, oddly shaped, white-walled apartment with plenty of quirks into a bright, comforting, feels-like-this-was-made-just-for-us home, where we felt love as a couple and a family.

Josh Davis

Introduction

"Mama, why do people stop us on the street to say they follow your blog?" My daughter Eleanor's question caught me off guard, as her petite four-year-old frame stretched over the armrest of our airplane seats, and she cuddled up to me as best she could while keeping her seat belt securely fastened.

Some thirty-three thousand feet up in the sky, I scrambled to respond. "That's a good question," I said, loosening my seat belt strap so I could face her better. I hadn't gotten far into my description of the internet, let alone blogging, before she lost interest and moved on to her panda sticker collection on the tray table in front of her. But her question had me thinking the remainder of the flight.

I started my blog in 2007, about a month before entering my senior year at the Juilliard School in New York City. I was twenty-one and newly married—the first married undergrad in the dance department since the program began in 1951, I was told. At the time I didn't know much about blogs, but the photo-friendly platform seemed the easiest way to upload pictures for my family many states away. It was also fun to write without having to capitalize anything. (Punctuation—who needs it?!) And, who doesn't love an alter ego? In the real world, I was more reserved. But online (cue superhero music), I shared more openly as *Taza*—a nickname my husband, Josh, who speaks Italian, jokingly called me because I'd drag him to tea parlors all around the city, collecting teacups even though we had zero space to store them. (Though I accidentally omitted one *z* from the original Italian *tazza*, and because of that letter subtraction, the once Italian word became a Spanish word. But the meaning remains the same: I am *cup*.)

As the year continued, the blog provided a new creative outlet for me, a welcome release, since I'd begun to dread each day in the dance studio—a burnout I never saw coming. After graduation, without the pressure of class, rehearsals, and performances, I focused on photography and writing, channeling all my creative energy into the blog.

It almost felt like a happy accident. Long before the birth of social media or brand partnerships, my little corner of the internet started to receive a couple million site visits each month from all around the world. I had no idea how it happened. I was just a girl in New York City blogging about day-to-day life, tracking my adventures in the form of brief letters, photo-heavy entries, and happy lists as I tried to focus on all the good things in the world, a coping mechanism that sometimes helped during challenging seasons.

More than a decade of posts later, I've leaned on this online community for support, love, and encouragement. They've laughed along as I've posted about mundane topics like whether to cut bangs (also when I've butchered mine) or when it's too soon to put up the Christmas tree (July, anyone?). But my readers also have walked with me through deeper, more personal moments, like when I shared my feelings as a new, exhausted, and lonely mother who was learning to love my postpartum body.

My readers have become an extension of our family, growing

with us from our newlywed years in our four-hundred-square-foot studio apartment in Harlem, through our move to DC and then back to our beloved New York City and beyond. Readers who have been with me as I became a new mother, and then a mother five times over. Readers who have been with our family as we've traveled the world and documented it all—from diaper blowouts in foreign countries to vomit on laps right before a six-hour cross-country flight. (In my dear carsick toddler's defense, it *was* a "very swervy taxicab ride" to JFK airport that day.)

My readers have joined my journey as a woman, wife, mother, and friend. Along the way, I've built some barriers, trying to protect my heart and the people I love. But I've also learned to tear down other walls, daring to trust the readers who've put their trust in me.

Now, with this book, I'm here to share even more with my online family and new friends about topics I haven't previously written about on the blog. This book includes essays on my infertility struggles, about growing up with an unhealthy relationship with my body, and about the time I questioned my faith, a cornerstone of my marriage and family.

I don't know why I didn't share these experiences in real time. Perhaps I wasn't sure I could find the right words for the heavy feelings weighing on me, or perhaps I worried I wouldn't be able to write well enough and thus would be misunderstood, or perhaps I was unsure of my own opinions as I navigated these experiences. Perhaps I was scared of confronting the thoughts and feelings I'd pushed back and shoved down deep inside.

But I (un)cover these stories in *A Coat of Yellow Paint* because they're important, because I feel more confident now than I did before, and because, while I hold these stories dear, I want them to help—and I'm hoping they can and will help—someone, somewhere. I've learned from both life and my blog that while opening my heart is difficult at times, sharing from my heart is the only way I want to share.

I never could have foreseen the incredible opportunities that my blog would bring our way, from the revenue that allowed Josh to resign from his job in financial services so we could focus on creating together and building *Love Taza* for six years, to the incredible flexibility that allows us to prioritize our family over work. But what I love most about my atypical career is what I've loved about it from the very beginning—the chance to share and connect with people near and far. I've felt so honored to reach out through this platform and build connections with *someone, somewhere.* And through my posts, I've hopefully found a way to inspire and encourage others to seek out the good, even on hard days, and love the life they live.

Eleanor is a few years older now and better able to understand what blogging means and what it is I do. Josh and I openly talk about all of it with our children, but today if she asked me why someone might stop us on the street and comment about my blog, I'd tell her it's because we are all connected. Because we have learned from one another in a very special and strange yet beautiful way. Because we're all going through this human experience together, and while our lives may look different, we all ultimately have more in common than not.

A Little Note on Noise

While blogging has certainly brought me some of my highest highs, being so exposed on social media has also brought me some of my lowest lows, especially when I give more weight than I should to the noise—that static noise, those frenetic piercing sounds, the incessant clamor, an annoying hum—all the different noises of life swirling around me.

Noise—and moving through it—is what much of this book is about.

As a once-upon-a-time dancer, I had to learn to decipher which music beats to follow and which to ignore as I moved across the stage. I've found this metaphor applies to life, too, as I've learned to focus less on the advice, comments, and criticisms—both online and in real life—that can cause me to miss a step.

I'm not here to tell you I've mastered tuning out the noise all the time. I wish! Some days it's still a lot for me too. "So why write an entire book about it?" you might ask. Well, publishing a book is one of my lifelong dreams (even if I did have to start capitalizing stuff and rein in my run-on sentences, which you know is not my strong suit, if you've ever followed my blog!). But I also hope that by sharing my own experience, I'll remind you of something you already know deep down: that your inner voice is yours for a reason. That you should dare to trust yourself and carve the path you want to walk in this life.

Through a lot of trial and error, I've learned a few tips and tricks about *tuning out* and *tuning in*. And I want to share those hard-earned insights with you. Why? Because I believe that whether you share on a public social media platform or live a private life with your guard held high, there is power and strength in trusting yourself. That after you do the research, say the prayers, and seek the counsel, you can turn inward and find the confidence to move through the noise with more love for yourself, and with greater peace and clarity.

When the noise interferes, I hope this book helps anchor you to the truth and hear your own voice again, reminding you that, apart from God, no one knows you better than *you*.

Thank you for sharing this experience with me. I'm holding back from using like seventeen exclamation points right now but want you to know it means so much that you've picked up my book. Thank you!!! (How about just three? . . . Is three okay?!) I'm cheering you on as you carve your own path, and I can't wait to see what you accomplish as you focus on what matters most: loving the life you live.

PART ONE

FEATHER YOUR NEST

DATE: somewhere between august 2012 and july 2017, with a day focused on december 17, 2014

 LOCATION: new york city

HAIRSTYLE: long with blunt bangs, to bleached platinum for a hot four months in the middle, back to long with blunt bangs by the end of this period

FAVORITE FOOD: is it bad i still love chocolate chip bagels from einstein's when i live a block away from zabar's on the upper west side?!

NUMBER OF LITTLES: mom of two! which turns into three at the end of 2014!

The View from a Fifth-Floor Walk-Up

"Five steps at a time," I told my husband, Josh, the words rushing between heavy breaths. I held my throbbing incision and tried to ignore the pain. The C-section was, after all, a small price to pay for our third bundle of joy.

When signing the lease on our fifth-floor walk-up two and half years earlier, I'd never imagined disliking these steep stairs as much as I did right then. We'd chosen the apartment as a place to launch the next chapter of our lives in New York City, and we'd been determined to make it work, stairs and all. But now with three kids in tow, including our newborn cradled safely in Josh's arms, I struggled more than ever to make it up those sixty-seven steps to the place our family called home.

"What are you thinking? An apartment without an elevator? All those stairs? With babies, with groceries, with a stroller? Not possible."

I'd heard these concerns more times than I could count. You know how when you tell someone you're pregnant, they often follow it up with, "Boy or girl?" Well, when you tell someone you've found a new apartment in New York City, people tend to ask, "Walk-up or elevator?" And then they usually add, "Walk-up? Are you crazy? How will you do that?!"

Josh and I weren't new to the city's culture. We'd previously lived in New York, both as singles and as newlyweds. But we'd spent three years in Washington, DC, before relocating to the Big Apple, now with two little ones along for the adventure—a bouncy nineteen-month-old toddler, Eleanor, with tiny pigtails in her soft hair, and our barely three-month-old baby boy, Samson, who beamed his wide, gummy grin that tore at my heartstrings in the best kind of way every time I saw it.

The choice to accept my husband's new job opportunity had been exciting for both of us, since we already knew and loved the city so much. While it did add a new level of nerves for us as young parents, we'd always been up for an adventure, and we felt good about the doors opening.

Less than a week after receiving the job offer, our family of four had spent three solid days exploring Manhattan and Brooklyn in search of the perfect rental. Josh's job started immediately, which meant we needed to find a lease that would begin midmonth. Three different real estate brokers made it clear our tricky timing would leave the options wanting.

We toured an apartment where the kitchen sink operated as part of the bathroom shower, and another rental that smelled of egg rolls at all hours of the day because a Chinese restaurant sat directly beneath. A beautiful, cool loft in Brooklyn that once served as a bowling-pin factory raised my hopes. But the catch— there's always a catch—was that the owner could potentially uproot us eleven months into our lease if she chose to return.

That meant she wanted to keep her furniture and décor inside the apartment while she was away. I felt like maybe I could do more with the whole kitchen-sink-inside-the-shower setup than come home to a stranger's bedding, clothes, and photos at the end of each day. We kept looking.

By day three, we still had no promising leads. Refusing to declare defeat, we homed in on the Upper West Side, broadening our search to include nearly anything that fit our tight schedule and budget. That's when we saw the fifth-floor walk-up on Amsterdam Avenue.

It was listed as a two-bedroom apartment, even though the second bedroom had no door and only three walls. Aside from that, we had to walk through each room to reach the next, as you would in a passenger train—thus the reason the real estate broker described the design as "a lovely railroad style."

From the mini refrigerator shelves to the even narrower front door, everything about the space—less than eight hundred square feet—felt *extra squished* together, as if we'd suddenly transformed into giants. I had no idea how we'd manage to get any of our furniture up those stairs, much less through the entrance. But with no better option, we signed the lease and made a leap of faith.

Soon we moved our family of four into the railroad-car walk-up and declared it "home." We installed a pressurized wall with a built-in sliding door to create the second bedroom, and during move-in day, Josh and I high-fived each other every time we maneuvered something through that front door.

I understood from the start that my perspective about the apartment's stairs and other quirks would either make or break this next chapter for us. Josh would be working long hours at the bank and traveling sometimes too. That meant it would come down to me trekking the stairs with the kiddos, alone, multiple times a day. So I told myself I'd do my best to never complain. We'd welcome those stairs into our daily routine, along with teeth brushing and handwashing, until they became habit. We'd make games of climbing them each day, getting my little ones excited until navigating those five flights became second nature to us all.

For me, it was easy to focus on the best part—location! Perched in the heart of the Upper West Side, our new home was nestled five flights above my favorite Thai restaurant, and later, a few years into our lease, our family's favorite bakery would take residency on the corner. The New York Public Library sat next door, Central Park waited just two avenues east, and Riverside Park along the Hudson was a short walk to the west. (I mean, it gave me an excuse to bust out *You've Got Mail* every single season!) I told myself I would concentrate on the fact that we were living in the center of my favorite city, which has this way of canceling out approximately three terrible things about itself for every magical encounter or experience it brings. And since the city had brought a lot of magical encounters and experiences my way, the terrible things were frequently being canceled out.

And so I chose to mentally highlight all the good things about the apartment. Like the charming view of the bustling city and the incredible dose of natural light each day, plus elegant crown moldings in the children's room and just enough counter space in the tiny kitchen to prop up my standing mixer while we whipped up homemade cookies. Besides, with sixty-seven stairs built into my new daily routine, I could consume all the homemade cookies I wanted. It was a win-win all around!

Sure, there were many moments when my arms were full of groceries and my little ones were fast asleep in the stroller as I stood in the building lobby, not sure what to do next. I admit I'd sometimes close my eyes and envision pushing the stroller into an elevator and straight into an apartment, where I could unload the groceries while the kids continued to sleep soundly. It was a simple dream of imagining no need to take multiple trips up and down five flights carrying babies and bags and sweating profusely in the process.

But nothing is ever completely, totally ideal. So I tackled each problem by reframing it as a challenge, each setback as an adventure. I learned to schedule our outings so that if my children did go down for their stroller snooze within the homestretch to our apartment building, I could take a detour to the Met Museum and treat myself to the European sculptures and the American Wing, admiring some of my favorite pieces of art while the babies napped in front of me. They'd wake up as we crossed through Central Park, just in time to see the spectacular skyline at the south end of the Great Lawn, with only two more avenues to go.

I snuck in many dates with Degas and Monet during those five years, all with sleeping kids in tow. I also learned to grocery shop so I could position the necessary haul under the stroller, working the goods like a jigsaw puzzle until everything fit just so. And once in my apartment lobby, I'd transfer it all into a single tote bag over my shoulder for the hike up the stairs.

I also got smart with services, like having bulkier items delivered to my door and sending my laundry out for wash and fold. Hey, if walking all those stairs with no laundromat in the building meant I didn't have to fold my fitted sheets (since I never properly learned how and would roll them into a crumpled ball anyhow), the trade-off wasn't so bad.

Over time, I saw the blessing the fifth-floor walk-up brought into my life—especially because my introverted nature meant I might have rarely left the house otherwise. The space was far too cramped for us to stay inside all day. Nudged out the door with my energetic crew, we were led to build new friendships, plan play-dates, and seek more adventures, taking advantage of everything the city had to offer.

In addition to the parks, museums, and activities, we grew to love the local bodega on the corner of Amsterdam Avenue. They had the best selection of ice cream pints—a major plus for a family that counts ice cream as its own food group. The bodega owners were particularly kind, displaying our children's drawings by their cash register and ordering DOTS candies for me when I couldn't find them elsewhere. That alone would've been reason enough to tolerate those five flights of stairs—and we haven't even talked about the bagels yet.

"Five steps at a time," I reminded Josh again as we neared the top of the stairs. I was so close, and sighting the finish line, I sensed nothing but excitement rush over me. Back home to my Eleanor and Samson, to where my heart dances with peace and pure joy, surrounded by my family. And where moments later, I stood at the window while rocking my new baby boy, Conrad, and admired what had become undoubtedly my favorite view of New York City—the view from our fifth-floor walk-up.

I have nothing but the fondest memories from that season of our lives. I'm proud of that young couple I see in the photos and home videos—carrying an oversized, bulky Christmas tree up the stairs once a year, working together to silently haul stroller seats with sleeping children up every flight, hosting parties with twenty-five friends having a good time in that tiny living room.

That apartment taught us countless lessons, from how to let go of things we didn't need to the importance of everyday physical activity. (Those daily climbs were better than any gym membership I've ever had!) But most of all, it taught us to find the good.

We can choose to fixate on the less-than-ideal parts of anything—a living situation, our weight, our packed schedules. Or we can shrug these off and focus on the actual perks,

> We can choose to fixate on the less-than-ideal parts of anything. Or we can shrug these off and focus on the actual perks.

feeling grateful for the kind neighbors who live next door, or the amazing things our bodies can do, or the fun events we have on the calendar. It all depends on the view.

DATE: a hot and humid morning in august 2004

LOCATION: new york city

HAIRSTYLE: jet black and so very short

FAVORITE FOOD: cheese pizza, please!

NUMBER OF LITTLES: pre-kids! but also college life, so the little sleep situation is basically same . . .

The Red Cowboy Boots

I took the red-eye flight alone from Salt Lake City, Utah, sixty miles away from the town of roughly one thousand people where I was raised. The plane landed at JFK a little before six in the morning, and since the dorm didn't open for move-in day until nine o'clock, I hung out at baggage claim for a couple of hours, plopped on top of my suitcases stacked three high while taking in the bustling airport scenery. I was the biggest ball of happy nerves, having not slept more than a handful of minutes the night before. The anticipation of moving to New York City and beginning my freshmen year at Juilliard had left me with an excitement that began in my somersaulting belly and traveled all the way down to my toes.

Speaking of toes, I was wearing baby-pink, midcalf, sheepskin boots. If you were around in the early 2000s, you might remember the ones. They were everywhere (usually in a tan or brown color, thanks to the UGG brand) and were worn with pretty much anything (denim cutoffs to sweatpants to you name it) in summer, in winter, in all the seasons. I'm sure many who wore the boots then (and now) enjoyed wearing them for many reasons, but I found them uncomfortable, with zero arch support and a whole lotta foot sweat. At the same time, with a heartbreakingly low amount of self-confidence in my body and appearance, I was desperate to fit in and belong, and I believed the trendy boot might do that for me. Make me popular? Make me cool? I could only hope.

At the airport I observed New Yorkers as they came and went from baggage claim, and I became self-conscious in my tall, fluffy boots that felt like a sauna around my feet. I didn't see anyone else in sheepskin boots. What if the boots weren't as popular in New York as back home, and since it was August, what if people thought a girl in these boots was silly? I scanned the crowd; the majority wore muted colors, mostly black. The internal dilemma began in my head. *Should I change? And not just my boots, but my entire outfit?* I went into the public bathroom and shoved myself and my suitcases into the handicap stall. Not sure *who* I was dressing for, or even *what* I was dressing for, I changed my outfit and my shoes a total of five times.

My first semester at Juilliard taught me many things. For starters, I learned an obscene amount of sex terminology and to steer clear of the hard-boiled eggs in the cafeteria. I learned the basics of proper posture thanks to the Alexander Technique, how to get by in a liberal arts class with a teacher who liked to poke fun at me and my religion by regularly referring to me as "Missy Mormon," and the power of a late-night improv session in a darkened dance studio and what it could do for one's soul.

But something that came into play for the first time in my life was seeing my peers and others around me happy and confident in their own right, while never morphing to fit either some sort of mold of the people around them or what others expected them to be. I'd spent many years thinking I had to style my hair a certain way, believe a certain way, talk a certain way to be seen. I'd spent a stupid amount of time (which—shoot!—I'll never get back) obsessing over things I didn't even like (hi, sheepskin boots) to appease random people whose names I can't even recall today.

This new frame of mind introduced by my peers was amplified every time I left campus and wandered the streets of New York. People wearing, eating, speaking, and creating a million different things. The best part? People didn't look twice at how I was dressed. People didn't care.

On weekends I went to Brooklyn, where I'd spend several hours in the company of vintage and thrifted beauties. From coats and dresses to hats and accessories, I was drawn to all the colors, the patterns, the textures. And while I still struggled plenty with my confidence and my self-worth—and with loving my body while surrounded by a campus full of unbelievably brilliant talent—I was grateful for the chance to find my own sense of style and experiment with this form of self-expression. For the first time, there in New York City, I realized there wasn't one mold to fit, and I quickly fell in love with breaking my old mold. I'm not saying that clothing can fix your problems, but I do believe expressing what makes you *you*, both inside and out, can do a lot for a person. It did for me.

> *I believe expressing what makes you you, both inside and out, can do a lot for a person.*

As autumn turned to winter, the sheepskin boots slowly made

their way to the back of my closet. Somewhere during this awakening of how fun and special and unique it was to just be *me*, I happened on a pair of old red cowboy boots during a day of thrifting in Brooklyn. Bright red, impeccable detailing, excellent condition. And what's even better, they fit the way I imagine Cinderella's glass slipper fit. (Am I the only one who usually has to do a little dance to get my feet and legs into most boots?)

I wore those boots out of the shop and into my everyday life with such affection. I wore them with my baby-doll dresses and my rehearsal sweats just the same. To the pharmacy and to special birthday dinners. On occasion, friends would playfully call me out about my boots, poking fun at them because they didn't really "go" as they might imagine boots to go. (A few years later, my mother-in-law was terrified I might wear them under my wedding dress. I didn't, though they did sneak into our wedding announcement photo!) With the boots came a sense of confidence. They made me happy, and that was good enough for me.

The newfound triumph my red cowboy boots sparked carried over into other areas of my life. When I entered my senior year of college as a newlywed, Josh and I decided to paint every wall in our new four-hundred-square-foot studio apartment in Harlem. We picked a pale yellow, a deep turquoise green, and a taupe color that my husband called "clay," plus a dark chalkboard wall in the entryway, because I've always had a thing for chalkboards. Four colors, for four hundred square feet made up of about seventeen walls, thanks to the odd-shaped apartment. I know it sounds like a bad idea, these colors in such a small space. "White walls will help everything feel more open and look bigger," more than one person kindly told us. And while that is absolutely true, for us, it wasn't so much about trying to make the space *bigger*—it was about making the space *ours*. Transforming the walls with color helped make that first mini-shoebox of an apartment into *our* first home.

And in each apartment since, we've transformed the spaces with paint, with color, with accented color, and with what makes us happy. Hot-pink sitting chairs, a bright-green wall next to a bold-blue one, and even the stretch of a long hallway in a deep navy.

When Eleanor and Samson were itty-bitty and we lived in the fifth-floor walk-up on Amsterdam Avenue, I turned our old brown piano into my all-time favorite color with a coat of yellow paint. During a time when white interiors and minimalist décor choices seemed to take on a life of their own via Pinterest and Instagram (with me being first in line to say what an admirer I am of all of the white and the minimalist take), I had learned over time, with my own experiences attached, that these choices were ours to make. Life is too short to pass up even the tiny things that bring us joy and inadvertently shape so much of our everyday. We can't get caught up in thinking we have to wear the sheepskin boots everyone else in our hometown is wearing instead of the red cowboy boots we actually gravitate toward and adore. We can't get sucked into thinking white walls are the only way, or that colored walls are the only way, or this or that or more of this . . .

"Your color choices make my eyes hurt," someone once commented on my Instagram, in reaction to the interior of my apartment. I thought, *But it makes my heart happy, and I'm the one who lives with this color choice, so we're both okay.*

A few years after I purchased my red cowboy boots, even with the repolishing and resoling and all the tender love and care I could muster, I'd worn the boots into the ground. And while parting ways with them felt almost tragic, I had learned in our shared time that I didn't need them to feel the sense of self-love and confidence they helped me find. It was there, with or without the boots. Love the life you live, with your shoe choice and wall color choice and all the much more important things in between. Because it's yours—and that alone is special.

DATE: a humid summer day in 2019

LOCATION: the very hot bathroom in our nyc apartment

HAIRSTYLE: wet and curly, first perm still going strong!

FAVORITE FOOD: manchego cheese with a side of green olives and are we in spain yet?!

NUMBER OF LITTLES: five little monkeys jumping on the bed!

The Soft, Doughy, and Warm Tummy

I plugged the blow-dryer into the wall while untangling my damp hair after taking my first hot shower in several days. While it was only a shower—with rubber duckies and floating boats and foamy alphabet letters surrounding my feet in the bathtub I shared with my family—in many ways, the shower felt as luxurious as a deep-tissue massage in some fancy spa where children aren't allowed. I snuck in a deep-conditioning treatment and shaved my legs, since no children had yet come to knock (bang?) on the bathroom door, and Madalena and Beatrice, thirteen months old now, miraculously continued to nap at the same time.

I had almost finished giving life to my wet hair when the sweat beading on my forehead from our poorly ventilated bathroom got to me. (In the next life, I think it wants to be a sauna.) I shut off the blow-dryer and stripped down to my bra and underwear while I finished my hair. Eleanor popped her head into the bathroom and said, "Can I sit with you?" I motioned her in with a smile and nod. My eight-year-old daughter hoisted herself onto the bathroom counter to hang with me as I finished getting ready for our day.

She touched my belly, where loose skin and dark stretch marks are permanent emblems earned from once housing life within, from being the first home to my five children. "Your tummy is so soft and doughy, Mama," she shared affectionately. "And warm."

In response to her innocuous comment, my thoughts automatically took me on a self-evaluating, split-second trip around my head. I visited particular conversations from both my childhood and more recent years, when those around me had analyzed and dissected my body. Then I saw a blitz of images and videos from the media I've consumed over my lifetime, content telling me what I should look like to be happy: what my waist measurement should be; what size my jeans, my dress, and my swimsuit should be; and what my postpartum body should look like. I visited the past diets and fads I'd unsuccessfully bought into at times, and briefly acknowledged the emptiness they'd always produced in those minutes and hours I spent obsessing over what I wish I could change about my body.

I didn't grow up in an environment where body positivity was a thing. And being a girl who spent most of her upbringing in a dance studio surrounded by mirrors while wearing pink tights, I was instructed daily to fixate on things I could not change about myself: my long torso and shorter legs, the way my hips lack the turnout required in the ballet world, and my large chest, which was supposedly "not good" for a dancer.

Keeping in mind that every woman has her own struggles and without casting judgment, I remember that when I was a teen, my mother signed up me and my sister (who is eighteen months younger than me) for weight loss programs like Weight Watchers and LA Weight Loss. Our body mass indexes were within normal range, but somehow that wasn't good enough for others. And with little knowledge of proper nutrition, I spent a portion of my teenage years carrying around a booklet where I wrote down everything I ate, adding each calorie consumed and then beating myself up over it.

I understand that the dance world strives for an ideal body type. I understand that many athletics and rigorous fields in the arts require the body to be an instrument that is fine tuned and exact. I get it. And I can appreciate it to an extent. It's the warping and manipulating and gutting measures often taken (and encouraged) to achieve that ideal that are difficult to wrap my head around.

The dance studio aside, an unhealthy relationship with my body followed me into adulthood. It festered its way into parts of my life where it had no grounds to go, into parts of my marriage and the early years of motherhood. I placed considerable value on the feedback I'd receive from others regarding my appearance, both before and after my first few babies. I sought validation from family, friends, and even strangers that I "got my body back" within the appropriate allotted time after giving birth, because the compliments helped maintain a front: if people liked how I looked, maybe they'd think *I* liked how I looked too. The validation helped briefly. Though it never seemed to stay as long as I needed it to.

While I liked and admired things about myself during this time, my body never made the list. I'd find ways to regularly revisit many confusing comments I'd received from past dance teachers and directors, as well as my own mother and peers over the years. *"Your broad shoulders are kind of manly." "What are we going to do about your weight?" "There is no definition between your calves and ankles." "Be careful—you easily put on muscle, and it makes you look big." "Do you have concealer tricks to cover her freckles?" "If you lost ten pounds, you would be better." "Dark turtlenecks can detract from your chest size." "What have you been eating lately? Your face has puffed up." "You just don't have 'the body.'"* Etc., etc., etc.

Over time the pain lessened when I revisited specific memories and phrases. Instead, a new numbness gathered where the hurt had once lived because somehow, unknowingly (or maybe a bit knowingly?), the experiences had paved the way in my head for *me* to be the most hurtful bully of all to *my* own body. I knew which phrases and words knocked me down the hardest, and I didn't think twice before repeating them in my head often.

I remember a moment during my pregnancy with Samson, in his final weeks inside my tummy, when he kicked and flipped with tremendous strength. I was nursing his big sister, Eleanor, about fifteen months old at the time, on the floor of her room, and I adjusted my seated position to relieve a cramping back when I caught a visual of myself in the full-length mirror propped behind the rocking chair. I saw my full, pregnant belly bursting out of my T-shirt, my hair slightly disheveled in a topknot, and dark-rimmed glasses on my face. I saw my first baby girl nestled into my side as she comfort-fed, while I supported her head burrowed into my chest. She played with the neckline of my shirt. I smiled at her and then smiled at myself in the mirror. I saw all of this, but I also saw something else I hadn't seen before: I saw my body as strong.

Thank you for being strong, body. Thank you for pushing through. Thanks for doing everything you're doing. I recited the words in my head as I looked at my reflection in the mirror. The entire moment felt a little out of body—talking to myself in this way and being kind to myself. A rush of love, though very brief, ignited in my thoughts and raced through my body. I held still, trying to understand it. It was the first time in a long time that I'd said something kind to myself about my body and truly believed it. And it was one of the best feelings ever.

Despite this affectionate encounter with myself, as time went on I struggled to consistently find that compassionate voice within me for my own body and manifest her again. I put on several masks in the interim low moments full of self-critique, from double sets of eyelash extensions to bleaching my teeth until the pain from sensitivity was too excruciating to handle. I coped as best I could while wrestling to love my body. My weight ebbed and flowed during the time around Conrad's birth. Every few months someone on the internet would analyze a recent photo from my blog or social media channels and message me, asking if I was expecting again. Each time it mortified me.

But then I caught myself doing the one thing I told myself I'd never do: complaining out loud to a girlfriend, while my children were present, about all the things I didn't like about my body. My strong body, my body that showed up for me again and again every day. My healthy and able body, which gave me years of dance without injury, a body that carried five babies full term and nourished them in the months and years that followed. A body that was strong, despite me dissing her often over ridiculous things like stretch marks, new wrinkles, a slowing metabolism.

I was mortified once again. But this time, it would stop here.

I'm raising three daughters and two sons in a world where we're bombarded with messaging around *all* the things, and especially our bodies. I accept that I make, and will continue to make, mistakes as I navigate my role in my children's lives, but I won't contribute to the chatter that breaks down the beauty and strength of our unique and special and individual bodies. Gifts from God that carry us through our minutes, our days, and our lives, and that we often take for granted. I know each child's relationship with his or her body will vary and may be trying at times. But as I choose to celebrate my own incredible body (though some days it's hard), I hope to share the important message of self-love, and that my intentional choice of words, when I speak to my littles of their own bodies as well as mine, will give them permission to build a confident relationship with themselves.

> I choose to celebrate my own incredible body.

Somehow, through working to help my children love their bodies, I've given myself permission to love my own. Acknowledging that my self-worth isn't based on anything but what's inside this body of mine. Pausing before I allow the negativity to seep into my head as I gaze in the mirror, and instead replacing it with anything but negative messages.

You are alive. You are healthy. You are strong. You are able to do hard things. You are beautiful. You are enough.

In the bathroom with Eleanor, I mentally conceded the existence of a small part of me that wanted to suck in my belly, pull away from my daughter's hand on my skin, and find an excuse for why Mama's tummy doesn't look like other tummies. Instead, I tapped into the love deep inside myself for me, loose skin, dark stretch marks, and all.

"Eleanor, isn't it so special?" I responded as I moved in closer to rub her back while she felt my tummy. "Isn't it so special what our bodies do for us every day? You were inside this tummy! Can you believe it?" We both had big smiles on our faces as she shook her head in disbelief and we looked at each other through the mirror.

"I love your warm tummy, Mama," she said as she nestled her head into my side while hugging me. I hugged her back.

I love it, too, Eleanor. I love it too.

DATE: the end of spring 2020

LOCATION: the hot and dry desert of arizona

HAIRSTYLE: all i know is, i packed a curling iron when we left new york city in march, but i haven't used it once.

FAVORITE FOOD: we need to talk about how good the mexican food is in the phoenix area. also, coconut creamer in my diet coke?! what is this goodness . . . ?

NUMBER OF LITTLES: five, with my tiny twins a few weeks away from turning two. their favorite pastime is pretending to blow out birthday candles in anticipation!

Spring of 2020

At the start of spring 2020, I downloaded a language app on my phone and set a goal of adding a few new Italian words and phrases to my vocabulary each day. I envisioned dressing my children in some pastel, springtime colors and what Josh's face would look like as I surprised him by casually exclaiming in Italian, *"Andiamo a fare un picnic sotto i fiori di ciliegio!"* (Translation: Let's go picnic under some cherry blossoms!) We'd frolic to the park, all seven of us, and merrily enjoy the inviting spring weather under a confetti of pink flowers raining from the trees.

It was a nice dream at the start of spring 2020.

Spring is almost over, and I haven't opened the new language app. We haven't gone on any picnics or seen any cherry blossoms in person. We haven't even admired the beauty that is spring.

I may not be learning Italian on the language app, but that's not to say my vocabulary isn't expanding. It *is*—just not how I anticipated. Along with many others around the world, my 2020 glossary of newly acquired language has broadened to include words like *coronavirus, COVID-19, social distancing,* and *multisystem inflammatory syndrome in children (MIS-C).* No daily practice of Italian pronunciation or diction is happening over here. And while words like *blossom* and *picnic* haven't been mentioned either, a whole barrage of words are being used each day that hadn't been in my daily vocabulary prior. You know the ones: *infection, virus, masks, curves, rates, immunity, antibody, vaccine,* and *remote learning,* to name a few.

Of course, there's lots of handwashing and plenty of wrangling my kids to do better handwashing. A great deal of sugar and soda have crept into our quotidian diets. (Remind me what a vegetable is again? Can an ice cream sandwich count as a lunch sandwich?) We mostly wear pajamas and sweatpants (although I *did* put on a springtime dress for a few hours on Easter Sunday). We aren't achieving much with the kids' schoolwork (read: I've given up entirely on the virtual-learning front), and I'm humiliated to admit how much we've upped the family's television intake as we've tried to rotate teaching school lessons, multitasking, and working and living in a strange state of limbo.

My mental health goes through moments of complete downward spiral, as I've questioned the choices I've made for our family (not only recently but over many years), as I've felt a lack of control over what's happening in the world and in my own life, as I've felt guilt for wanting to keep my family safe and healthy during this crazy time—and been overwhelmed by the repercussions of doing so publicly.

Instead of bright and airy, spring 2020 has been incredibly dark and at times suffocating. For many, it's been full of tragedies, as hardships and consequences spread across the world in response to the pandemic known as COVID-19, leaving so much uncertain, unfair, and confusing.

You have to be strong for your kids. You need to stay. You need to go away. You should make this time magical for your children. You should take on a new hobby, read more books, explore recipes in the kitchen, serve your community, friends, and neighbors more during this time.

What if I can't find my strength? What if the tidy and happy home, the hobbies and recipes and book reading, the service opportunities and magic of childhood I once was capable of creating are being strangled in a cycle of negativity and uncertainty and confusion I don't yet know how to break?

I tell myself to hold it together, but this admonition usually makes me feel worse. I crouch between my sleeping babies, Beatrice and Madalena, and stroke their heads and tickle their backs as they doze to sleep in their low-lit room. I do all in my power to fight back the fear steadfastly consuming me and now reaching a tipping point because it is dark, and the children are asleep, and my body and mind realize they can expel the tears more freely. I hum the children's song "I Am a Child of God" one last time to my sleeping girls, a song we sing together every evening after our bedtime prayers. I don't know if it will help, but I am desperate and hopeful. It helps a little.

But the thing is, I'm still in a funk. I haven't entirely pulled through, and at times this makes me feel a bit like an imposter, proclaiming to the world the beauty of moving through the noise and loving life, when some days I'm succumbing to the heaviness of the racket and clamor from a frighteningly loud world. Sometimes I wish we all had detailed, step-by-step instructions on how to get through every type of crisis—whether a private problem or a public pandemic—and their ripple effects.

"What is one thing—just one—that made you smile today?" Josh asked me recently as I shared my frustrations and failures with him while openly sobbing. I fell for his restorative question without even realizing it.

"Well," I thought out loud, "all the kids were laughing so hard earlier, and that made me happy . . . and I changed some words to a song we were singing . . ." Because when the word *poop* is added to anything, my kids lose it. I proudly take credit for their love of slapstick, though I'm less inclined to take ownership of their potty-humor obsession. Poop jokes aside, I kept my answer going. "And Conrad and I had a *Sound of Music* sing-along this afternoon, which was a lot of fun. We finally got all the words right to the third verse of 'My Favorite Things' . . . and I played this game with the twins where they kept marching in circles around me, and I'd occasionally reach my arms out and tickle one of them. They couldn't stop laughing! It was so much fun."

Before I knew it, I wasn't crying anymore but was savoring a small burst of joy. I kept coming back to it later in the day, when I felt myself slipping into more fear, more self-doubt, more negativity.

> But when I acknowledge I can't find all my strength right now, perhaps a bit of strength will bloom, like a small cherry blossom.

Maybe this time with less fortitude will last longer than is ideal, but maybe that's okay, too, because it's a chance to practice being brave. It'd be nice to have everything in order (plus an expanding Italian vocabulary), but sometimes not everything can be in order, and much is out of our control.

Sometimes we aren't strong enough and aren't sure if or when we will be.

But when I acknowledge I can't find all my strength right now, perhaps a bit of strength will bloom, like a small cherry blossom. Because when 2020 robbed spring from the world and everything feels uncertain, I can hold on to the giggles and tickles and sing-alongs. After the next poop joke concludes, I intend to bring all five of my babies in for a tight hug. And in that moment, my babies and their giggles are what I'll keep holding on to. For now, I'm grateful for the sliver of strength they gift me—by way of soothing, extraordinary, and uplifting joy.

PART THREE
IT TAKES TWO TO TANGO

DATE: an evening in the spring, 2006 (with the paper-towel scene taking place sometime in 2010)

LOCATION: big nick's pizza joint just off 71st and columbus

→ **HAIRSTYLE:** reddish highlights in shoulder-length brown hair

FAVORITE FOOD: frequenting my favorite francesco's pizzeria on 68th and columbus weekly, so almost feels strange we went to big nick's on this night!

NUMBER OF LITTLES: just two lovebirds in the good ol' days, when we should have been stocking up on sleep instead of investing so many hours in watching every single episode of lost

The Paper-Towel Tantrum

It felt different from the very beginning. I'm not talking about love at first sight, or dramatic butterflies in my belly, or even this sense of *he's the one*. (A funny sidenote worth mentioning is that it took six more months before anything turned the slightest bit romantic.) It felt different because it felt . . . real. Straight off the bat, first night out. No fluff or trying to impress or shuffling around topics to make ourselves look good (I mean, maybe a *bit* of trying to look good).

It was the kind of real you get only when you step out from behind the concrete walls built over the years to protect yourself. And not just step out but tear the walls down as you do so. The whole thing. All four walls plus the top and bottom, which may still hide some of your layers. Only then can you truly, finally get *real*.

This is what happened when I met Josh.

I can pinpoint the time and place. I can see his young, scruffy, handsome silhouette across the table from me at that little pizza and burger spot on West 71st Street. We were college students at separate schools in the city. We had two short conversations prior to our first date: one thirty-second introduction by the elevator at the church we both attended; the other maybe a minute longer at a friend's party a few weeks later. But here we were, with pizza propped in front of us and a soccer game blaring on the TV to our side. He wore a deep navy jacket with the collar popped in the back, and he spilled three glasses of water while we sat there together. (Perhaps that's what endeared him to me forever, but I suppose that's a story for another time.)

Our first proper get-to-*really*-know-you conversation went differently than I'd ever expected it would go. Him, asking a question I'd been asked countless times before, and me, a split second before I answered it as I had always answered it—almost robotic at this point—responding with an entirely new answer. The sincere answer, the answer I'd never articulated to anyone. Ever. I felt vulnerable yet empowered in that moment. I didn't even know this man, but it felt like I was talking to someone I'd known and trusted and loved my entire existence. I know, I know. It all sounds so very corny and ridiculous (are you even still reading this?!).

Within the hour, my walls had all come down. Our conversation moved freely and quickly into territory that usually took me months to reach after meeting someone for the first time. That's when I knew this was different. At the time, communication was not my strong suit, and I still have to diligently work on it each day. Up until that point, I hadn't seen many examples of what a healthy conversation looked like between two people who loved each other, and I could be skeptical when someone presented their ideas and thoughts in a kind way.

Roughly thirteen years and five children later, I practically pinch myself each day at how Josh has made this partnership my safest refuge, a judgment-free zone where open, loving, and respectful communication has always been top priority. That's not to say we don't have our share of arguments. We've both lashed out and said hurtful things over the years. We've even raised our voices. But learning and practicing to put our pride aside and be gentler, more trusting, more selfless, more forgiving—has been 100 percent worth the work.

When we were newly married and living in Washington, DC, we went shopping at a nearby Costco on a busy Saturday. After unloading all the bulky items from our cart into the compact trunk of our light-yellow VW Beetle convertible, we realized we weren't fighting the usual battle to get everything squeezed in just right—we'd forgotten a few key items on our shopping list. Josh volunteered to run back into the store and grab the items while I pulled the car around to the front. About twenty minutes later, I parked our Beetle at the entrance, and Josh hopped in with our second haul of goods and the most ecstatic expression on his face. He held a twelve-pack of jumbo paper-towel rolls on his lap and beamed. "I got the ones with these little flowers on them for you! Do you love them?"

The disapproving expression on my face must not have been clear, because he continued, "See right here—squiggly flower patterns!"

I thought he must be joking. The paper towels were covered in colorful flowers. Yes, we were at Costco, which means things come in bulk, but we'd never bought this massive pack of paper towels before. But that wasn't even the main issue. I couldn't get past the fact that these weren't plain, white paper towels. Plain, white paper towels were all I'd ever brought into our home for the prior three years of marriage, and maybe he'd never noticed, but I believed he was doing this to spite me.

"Oh my gosh, Josh! Are you kidding me? These are ridiculous. And now we have twelve jumbo rolls of them! These are so ugly! Uuuuggghhh. I can't believe this. These are *ugly*! *Are you serious?!*"

I know my response doesn't make me look good. Sharing this makes *me* sound ugly. Spoiled. Even a brat? Totally a brat. Nevertheless, I went off. Over a twelve-pack of flowery-patterned paper towels (even if the packaging did advertise, with screaming block letters along the side, how its rolls had twice as much paper as regular rolls, claiming to equal a twenty-four pack of regular floral-print rolls for just the two of us to work our way through over the next twenty years—block letters that popped out bigger and bolder every time I glanced in Josh's direction). I didn't shut up about it until we'd been on the freeway for several minutes.

It took ten more minutes of driving before I realized how ridiculous I'd been. And it took about three more hours before I put my pride aside and apologized for being so obnoxious about something that didn't matter.

But you know how Josh responded? He never lashed out at me, even as I lashed out at him over and over again (finding ways to slide other frustrations into the conversation too—because I'm really good at that and because hashtag-old-habits-die-haaaaaaarrrrrd). Instead, he accepted my apology straightaway and brought me in for a big hug. He didn't mention the flower-patterned paper-towel situation again, even though he could have poked fun at my overly dramatic reaction then and all the months that followed, thanks to our twenty-four pack—and even in the years to come.

His response is something I admire greatly about him. The

way he phrases and articulates things in such a gentle way and moves on in a loving way too. I've especially admired this as we've brought children into our home, because their eyes and ears are always open and soaking up how Josh and I interact with others and each other.

Communication is key. We hear this a lot when it comes to relationships. But I'd say *kind* communication is key. And sometimes that's tricky when you're so close to someone, when you know which buttons to press, when that person is your best friend but at the same time irks you more than anyone else on the planet. Kind communication is an elevated level of communication.

It's taken time and a lot of conversations for me to break old patterns that went something along the lines of "You always do this!" or "You never do that!" or "Why can't you be more like this?!" I strongly believe that delivering a message with a healthier approach like "I really appreciate when you do this for me, and it's hard for me when this happens instead" or "Do you think we could try it this way next time?" not only benefits our relationship but also benefits our children. The way we each communicate with our

Kind communication is an elevated level of communication.

spouses trickles down into the way we communicate with our kids, and then how they communicate with one another. Speaking negatively carries consequences our children will have to deal with, even long after they're grown and flown from the coop. I know firsthand the journey to overcoming unhealthy models, and believe me when I say that our words, our tone, our interactions with our loved ones matter. They matter a lot.

Let me be clear: While this is what we strive for, Josh and I aren't perfect. But removing sarcasm while not belittling or imitating each other with exaggerated or loud voices has helped us remain calm, listen more intently, be heard ourselves, and feel more loved through the course of conversation.

Marriage is complex and so very personal. But we only know what we know. And until Josh came into my life, I didn't know this different way, this better way, this respectful way, was even an option. I'm learning to let the small things go, the quirks and odd habits that don't need fixing. I'm learning to overlook the fact that the *extra*-wide tennis shoes he insists on ordering for our children aren't as cute as the ones I'd have picked out, and instead I appreciate that he's so passionate about their shoe width and protecting their tiny straight toes from getting squished and curved (I mean *who* thinks of these things?). And while I sometimes wish he hadn't become a healthier eater in his thirties (couldn't he at least have waited until his forties?!), because it is not as fun to order dessert for one on date nights, I try to acknowledge it's great that he prioritizes his nutrition and brings a conscientious approach to healthy meals into our household.

We all have the ability to frequently acknowledge the strengths our partners bring into our relationships, and at the same time we can share our frustrations without seeking to hurt their feelings. We can choose to be a team, true partners who will forever have each other's backs and be the biggest cheerleaders our partners will ever know. And we can apologize. When we've said something cruel or pushed an issue too far (or not far enough), we can fess up and make amends and say we're sorry. Truly, genuinely sorry. Because we all make mistakes (like losing it over floral-print paper towels), and we'll continue to make them. That's the easy part. The hard part is finding the strength inside ourselves to do better next time, communicating our remorse in the most loving way, and healing the hurt for all involved.

Perhaps even more importantly, we can also accept the apology when it's our turn to do so and choose to Let. It. Go. This is easier said than done at times, but it's worth it. Always worth it.

DATE: early february 2011 (and a brief spring morning in 2015)

LOCATION: our home on capitol hill and then eastern market, washington, dc

→ **HAIRSTYLE:** long and dark, with bangs almost grown out so i can tuck them behind my ear!

FAVORITE FOOD: no longer pregnant but still craving mcdonald's big macs and breakfast burritos (i know, i know . . .)

NUMBER OF LITTLES: eleanor, our first, is just a few days old . . . we're still drunk off that sweet new-baby smell

Dads Who Do Diapers

Josh arched back and clasped the buckle of the baby carrier between his shoulder blades, snuggling Eleanor to his chest in one effortless motion. It took a total of two seconds. *Click.*

I was instantly annoyed.

Having given birth to Eleanor days earlier—when the doctor had thrown my detailed, three-page birth plan to the wind, tossing all my dreamy expectations right along with it—even the idea of standing up straight felt not only impossible, but excruciatingly painful as my C-section stitches stretched and laughed at the thought. Earlier that day after taking our baby girl for a walk, I'd spent a full twenty minutes trying to unlatch the same damn buckle, which resided in that impossible-to-reach place in the middle of my back. Once we made it home, I'd given my best effort to removing the carrier without disturbing Eleanor, bending to the front and to each side, trying to twist the carrier to the left and then the right. But no matter how hard I tried, I couldn't reach the buckle. And the pain had grown intense!

I'd even considered heading outside to find a stranger to help me. Eventually, with our beloved firstborn attached to my chest—and now screaming bloody murder—I *finally* found a solution by lying on the bed. Miraculously, this helped with the gravity and eased the pain, freeing us both from the carrier just in time.

Then here he was, the husband, the dad—two seconds and *bam!*

I bit my tongue as we left the apartment for an evening walk together. Our daughter slept soundly, pressed safely against her papa's chest. I embraced the short break, since until that moment she and I had been bonded through every waking and sleeping minute of her life. For the most part, I loved mothering. I loved her. I loved it all . . . but still, I admit, the break was nice, especially because of my pain.

Together, we made our way to Eastern Market, a beautiful brick terminal built in 1871, full of stalls where local vendors sold groceries and all sorts of goods. Josh and I briefly wandered in different directions, picking up various items as we each made our rounds. I took my time passing the pastries and then made a stop by the flower section before finding Josh again a few rows ahead. When I approached, several people were peeping a look at our sleeping daughter. They smiled big in the direction of my husband. "Aww, what a good dad!" a woman said ever so fondly as she passed. Then she repeated, "You're such a good dad!"

Maybe the hospital drugs hadn't fully worn off, maybe exhaustion had set in, or maybe my shifting hormones had gotten the best of me and darkened my mood because he'd buckled the baby carrier with the ease of flipping a light switch. But whatever the reason, I was bothered. *He's "such a good dad" because he's carrying his own baby?* Sure, it was nice to see him getting a compliment. But why in the world would carrying our baby merit such praise for a man when women do this all the time without so much as a nod of approval?

Once again, I decided to let it go. I didn't want to be negative, and I wondered if I was making a big deal of it in my head. After all, Josh was a great dad, and parenthood shouldn't become a competition of who's doing more, sleeping less, receiving better compliments. But thirteen years and five kids later, I'm here to report that any time my husband's out with our children, there's *still* this sort of surprise—even shock—from many around us. It's often followed by admiration and immense amounts of vocal praise.

Why do strangers react this way when they see Josh with our kids? Maybe because they're not used to seeing a father out in the world with his own children. Because in many ways, outdated stereotypes have created this brew of toxic masculinity, with faulty messages that sound a bit like this: *A man can't possibly nurture the way a woman can. Raise your boys to be masculine, to have egos, to be better than women, to make more money, to hold better titles, to be the alpha . . .* It's all *super* healthy! (That last sentence is sarcastic, in case you couldn't tell.)

Not all men are this way, of course. While we were living on the Upper West Side of Manhattan, the playgrounds and parks were often full of dads enjoying time with their kids, many of whom we've gotten to know. Many men are attentive, active, and fully present in the moment as they focus on being great fathers any chance they get. Some take part in school drop-offs or pick-ups and are also juggling work as they co-parent with their spouses. Like Josh and I, they believe in the importance of the father being a team player to make a family unit thrive.

Several years after Eleanor's birth, shortly after Josh had

resigned from his job at the bank to work full-time at home along-side me, we were still tag-teaming the care of two active toddlers and our newest baby, Conrad. During this sleep-deprived chapter of life—when our two-year-old and three-year-old loved waking up before the sun every day (Even on weekends! Where in heaven do we send the memo to get kids to snooze on the weekends?!)—we were on a trip with extended-family members when I overheard one of them say something I wasn't supposed to hear.

I'd been up until about one in the morning writing and editing photos for the blog, and then I'd spent the remainder of the night nursing and comforting tiny Conrad as he fought off a fever. When six in the morning had barely rolled around, our *very* alert older two, Eleanor and Samson, were already up and at it. Josh didn't think twice as he happily took the first shift with them, heading outside to play and grab breakfast. He returned around eight o'clock with well-fed children who had shed their morning energy.

I was up again by then, sitting just behind the closed door of our hotel room editing more photos while Conrad, finally feeling better, slept beside me. That's when, on the other side of the door, the family member said to Josh, "We're concerned about all you're doing for her, Josh. You're doing too much."

Even now, I feel hot reliving it. My husband repeatedly tried to cut off the comments by defending me and our situation, but this family member kept pushing, surely assuming I couldn't hear.

One of the hardest things for me, with the unique setup that Josh and I have created over the past several years, is breaking through the norms of what is considered appropriate. To past generations, especially among more traditional thinkers, I should have been the one to wake up with my children before six in the morning, gathering their breakfast and then perhaps bringing some in for my husband. How odd that he, their father, should wake with the children and take the first shift of being, what's the word . . . a parent?

Perhaps we don't give men enough space to explore what incredible fathers they have the potential to be. Members of our society often joke about men being "the babysitters" when they're left alone with their children, suggesting the kids will be fed poorly, become filthy, and bounce off the walls. Of course, many men buy into this falsehood because we help push that messaging forward. I once witnessed a friend ask her husband for help with their two young babies. It was a Saturday morning, when he didn't have to go to the office. As she relayed a short list of things while handing over the diaper bag, he interrupted by throwing his hands up in frustration and saying, "No way. I don't do diapers!"

His reaction confused me. It also broke my heart.

I understand that many jobs are demanding, and not everyone has the flexibility Josh and I have built into our schedules. The long hours and work-life culture often don't allow for prioritizing family time. But I've seen many men (and women) find a healthy balance by making the moments they do have with their families count: one parent prioritizes being home for dinner with their kids even when it means going back to the office shortly after; another volunteers for field trips; another coaches Little League games. When with their loved ones, they put the phone away, turn off the TV, and ignore the emails, determined to treasure their time together.

Every family structure is unique, and every relationship requires adaption, teamwork, and sacrifice. And yes, it's an absolute privilege for any family to find the time and resources to regularly focus attention on one another.

But perhaps *all* of us aren't doing enough to acknowledge that men can and should have a more active responsibility in their role as fathers. The confidence, character building, and love it brings to everyone involved makes a lasting impact—if we choose to break free of the stereotypes and let dads be dads.

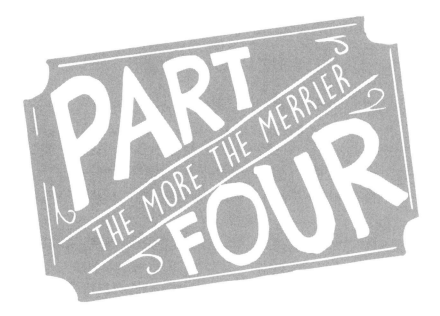

DATE: a few days after my birthday, 2009

➔ **LOCATION:** washington, dc

HAIRSTYLE: long and brown with a prenatal vitamin that was making it shine like its job!

FAVORITE FOOD: georgetown cupcake, for breakfast, lunch, and dinner, thanks

NUMBER OF LITTLES: none ⬅

The Repetitive Birthday Wish

The bright flame from the candle flickered and danced on top of my birthday cupcake. With shredded coconut flakes atop a big, swirly glob of cream cheese frosting, my birthday treat balanced in the palm of my hand, held close to my lips, as Josh finished singing. It took me half a second to make my birthday wish. I closed my eyes and blew out the flame.

I loved birthdays. And I loved cupcakes. (Still do, on both accounts.) And while this birthday had been magical in its own right—we'd been in the sunny Dominican Republic on my actual birthday the week before—this whole making a wish after singing the traditional song was a cruel reminder that I'd completed another 365 days around the sun and was no closer to the wish I obsessed over each day: a pregnancy, a baby. It was my twenty-third birthday.

About a year and a half later, four months before my twenty-fifth birthday, Eleanor—with a head of dark hair accompanied by the sweet smell of heaven—was born thanks to the assistance of in vitro fertilization (IVF). If you're unfamiliar with IVF, it involves a lot of medications, several needles, and self-administered shots.

You go under anesthesia while the doctors retrieve your eggs, and then, after they combine one with the father's sperm, they implant one or more embryos (joining your nerves and anxiety, and all the hopeful prayers you can muster). It's rather invasive, expensive, and not much fun. But it's the procedure for which I'm forever grateful, as it helped fulfill birthday wishes back then and years down the road too.

Josh and I married two days after my twenty-first birthday. Sure, I was young and hadn't yet clocked in the years of life experience some might believe are a prerequisite for marriage, but I knew Josh was my person, and I was ecstatic to carry on life with him by my side. To this day, it's still the best decision I've ever made.

Discussions of babies and starting a family were always at the forefront of our marriage. Several conversations when we first met centered around the topic of family. Josh wasn't shy about voicing how much he looked forward to being a father and having lots of children. I loved that about him (and still do). This brought us together back then and to this day. When we have disagreements or frustrations, whatever the subject, our synced beliefs about prioritizing family have always centered our relationship.

Trying for a baby wasn't something we decided on lightly, especially since I was in my last year at the Juilliard School and had been on a rather direct path since childhood toward a career in the professional dance world upon graduation. But there are fewer than a handful of times when I feel I've been given clear guidance to pursue a specific path, and as I chose to pursue marriage and beginning a family at the ripe old age of twenty-one, I felt immediate peace and purpose in my decision.

One year passed by. Then two.

The longest two years. In many ways, the hardest two years. While I now know that many women have to endure the waiting far longer and often never see their desired end result—an experience whose magnitude I can't possibly comprehend—at the time it was as though my insides were being torn apart, month after month, with no sign of a baby. In retrospect, I thought it would take only a few months to get pregnant—an expectation no one in my life had ever countered. That I was in my early twenties compounded my perplexity, since for many years as a dancer, I'd been in tune with and had command over my capable body, which I felt was now suddenly failing me.

Perhaps the hardest part for me was feeling alone through it all. The times I attempted to share my struggle with the people closest to me, I frequently heard dismissive commentary, often masked as care or concern. *"Naomi, you're so young." "You have so much time." "Why would you even want that right now?"* (Actual things people said to me during those two and a half years of wishing I was pregnant.) Because I was young, most of my dear friends weren't even in serious relationships, let alone married. My current chapter of life already looked vastly different from theirs, and my fertility questions added a new degree of isolation, with no one to relate to or understand my longing.

One particular encounter happened with a friend a few months before our college graduation, as we discussed our rehearsal schedule for the week—nowhere near the subject of family planning. "Naomi, tell me you're on the pill and not thinking about babies already," she said, so out of the blue, so *accusatory.*

I tried to deflect. "Where did that come from?" I responded. And playfully trying to take all the eyes off me, "Why, are *you* thinking about babies?!"

With little understanding and support from my closest friends and family (I thank the handful of people who were there for me—they know who they are), I started to feel almost embarrassed that I was longing for something the world around me wouldn't acknowledge as legitimate because of my age. I grew tired of defending my hopeful desire to become a mother and raise a family, just because I was *young*. Through my few encounters where the topic was poorly received, I learned to compartmentalize it when interacting with others.

A couple of years into our unsuccessful attempts at having a baby, Josh and I shared breakfast with newlywed friends who were older than us. I blinked back tears and tried to match our friends' excitement level when their news was shared, while Josh softly squeezed my hand under the table. "We weren't even trying!" she started. "We've only been married a couple of months!" I wanted to be happy for them; however, I was starting to feel everything but.

During those years I found a lot of community in the blogging world (before the explosion of social media). My blog became a helpful distraction for my head, as I shared "happy lists" and invited readers to share their own happy lists with me. I'd publish several of the lists on my blog, in between the Polaroid adventures and little letters and life-lately photo roundups. I did my best to focus on the good, the fun, the life around me that I loved. After all, I had much to appreciate, and we were happy. On occasion, I'd surf the internet for anyone talking about having infertility problems in their early twenties, but my search was unsuccessful.

I sometimes wondered if I should publicly talk about what I was experiencing. Maybe it would help? Not only me but someone else out there too? But . . . I couldn't do it. I knew deep down that I wouldn't be able to handle it—the world weighing in on something so fragile, something so misunderstood even by those who knew me in real life. I can't say with certainty, but based on my experiences in the online space over the past decade, I believe sharing about my infertility struggles in real time would only have added another layer of noise and frustration to my pain. Also, I hadn't acquired the tools I now have to dismiss the noise. In a way that's hard to articulate, I know talking about it would have broken me.

After about two years of unsuccessfully trying to conceive, Josh and I turned to modern medicine for answers. That led us to IVF and the blessing of Eleanor joining our family a little over a year later. While we were grateful the process resulted in our baby girl, it wasn't all smooth sailing. We had difficulties along the way, with an early miscarriage before IVF, an alarming number of painful cysts developing on my ovaries after the first egg retrieval, and then the loss of an implanted embryo during the first trimester. While acknowledging all of that, I still had a healthy baby in my arms at the end of the process. I'd been handed the world, along with a strong dose of joy, peace, and complete love.

Then my body gave me the most unexpected, happy miracle when Eleanor was only seven months old. I found out I was pregnant, without any fertility intervention, with our strong mister Samson. And a few years after that, as we scheduled a meeting with my OB in anticipation of needing help conceiving again, our silly mister Conrad showed up, which felt like a second miracle. While at times the process felt easy (getting pregnant when you have a seven-month-old baby, like, *hello*!), the experiences before and after our fertility journey weren't always as simple.

But as the years passed and our family grew times three, I

gained more confidence in myself and the uniqueness of my story. I wanted to share with others what the road had looked like leading up to our present day. Almost unwittingly, when Conrad was a few months old, I shared a couple of sentences around the subject in a blog post. In a piece about breastfeeding, I blogged that nursing now came more naturally and "has made me feel very grateful, especially since other aspects of having kids [haven't] come easily." I went on, "For example, I'm not one of those lucky ladies who blinks and suddenly is pregnant, or has had birth experiences I have all loved."

The comments section of this blog post, which quickly filled with dozens of visceral reactions from women around the globe, proved that fertility, and anything surrounding it, was complex and sensitive territory. My heart broke all over again—for the readers' experiences and pain and for how some women harshly discredited my experiences and pain.

Here's what time and personal growth and life in general have taught me: Other women, whether I know them in my life or online, have no say in how I should feel about my story. And they have no say in how *you* should feel about *your* story either. It's *my* story for a reason. And it's *your* story for a reason. We can't let the noise from others' opinions create interference with our inner compass. And while it is absolutely easier to say than do, never allow someone else to pressure you to compartmentalize your pain,

> We can't let the noise from others' opinions create interference with our inner compass.

or worse, not feel the pain at all. Yes, someone else's pain may indeed be greater, bigger, and ever so present, but that does not invalidate yours.

In recent years, I've observed a shift in conversations happening both in person and online—and it inspires me. Women around the world are courageously opening up the vulnerable discussions around fertility. Women are sharing their struggles to conceive after a year, or ten years; with secondary infertility and the differing ways that might look; with exploring and undertaking foster care and adoption and pursuing what they know is their path, regardless of the naysayers. Their sharing has helped me—as I've felt tremendous isolation and pain around this topic, as well as shame and guilt for ever trying to voice it—understand how my birthday wish at twenty-one years old, at twenty-two years old, at twenty-three years old, was not absurd and ridiculous. Striving to grow our family and experiencing secondary infertility while having the same birthday wish over several years was also not absurd and ridiculous.

I hope we can continue to make more room in the world for the stories around fertility, and especially for the stories that look different from ours. I hope we can allow women everywhere to keep making their birthday wishes—whether it's wishing to expand their families or expand their careers, or wishing for a good hair day or a good night's rest, without the chatter of everyone else's opinions keeping them awake.

Make that birthday wish, friend. I'm rooting for it to come true.

DATE: like, every night of 2019

→ **LOCATION:** our kitchen table

HAIRSTYLE: short, which is quick to style and great, except that i have to style it every day ←

FAVORITE FOOD: not one of the same seven or eight dinners our family seems to have been rotating through over and over and over for the last one thousand nights

NUMBER OF LITTLES: fiiiiiive

The Case for the Loud Dinner Table

I don't want to name any names, but at one point during the meal, a handful of spaghetti noodles drenched in marinara sauce flew across the table. Five little ones erupted in laughter as two of them stood on their chairs and shook their bums at each other. I raised my voice in a distressed attempt to rein in the mayhem that infiltrated our meal. It wasn't my first rendezvous with this bunch, so I knew this sort of silly-chaos is often followed by full-blown tears, since someone is likely to get hurt.

"Sit down, or you might fall," I said sternly, one child bum in the air now wiggling in my direction. "Sit dow—" I hadn't completed my words before said bum rocketed into the air and smacked down on the hardwood floor beside the table. And then, tears. So many tears. Wanting to emphatically shout, *"Told you so!"* I instead held my child close, marinara sauce now smeared on the shoulder of my shirt and clumped all over my lap.

If our dinner table excels at one thing, it's being loud. Messy too. But mostly loud. For the longest time, I'd aggressively shush everyone every three seconds or so when voices grew elevated, silliness progressing, until I realized this was only solidifying my epithet of "annoying mother" and nothing else. And while it might be hard to comprehend, with talk of flying noodles and bums shaking high in the air, during each meal Josh and I were working diligently to instill table manners in our kids' core habits. But after all, they were just that—kids. And I didn't want to entirely squash my longtime mantra to *let them be little*.

After brainstorming ways to reel in the madness that commenced each meal, Josh and I began incorporating games into our dinners, and we also found having conversation starters with fun prompts especially helpful. The kids would be still as we'd explore feelings and share stories based on different categories:

"If you had a superpower for a day, what would it be?"

"What is the greatest invention?"

"Pretend you are popcorn popping!"

We'd also learn some of the most endearing facts about our kids and each other.

Conrad hopped off his chair and rounded the table, demonstrating his superpower, speed. He was rather fast even without the help of his superpower and, thanks to a comment during his dinner demonstration, was convinced for several weeks after that he was blurry when he ran.

Samson defended his belief that invisibility cloaks are the greatest invention of our time, even if they haven't yet been invented. As for the popcorn shapes, take my word for it when I say the popcorn kernels are sassy and adorable, complete with hip popping and scrunched eyebrows and sly smirks that give popcorn a whole new meaning.

A few months later, Josh drew a question from our box of prompts as our family ate pork chops with potatoes and broccoli. With more A.1. Steak Sauce smeared across our white table than on the actual plates, plus a good pile of broccoli on the floor, where Beatrice apparently was manifesting a dog to help get rid of the mini vegetable trees on her plate, I was over the dinner-table scene. I looked across our open kitchen, where four of the six doors to our top kitchen cabinets remained open, and tried to avoid looking at the sink of overflowing dishes from the night before. The day had been long, yet the dinner shift felt longer.

I glanced at my husband, whose face looked just as tired, while he read the question aloud: "What is your favorite time of day?" The kids started calling out different time stamps from their twenty-four-hour blocks, from recess to snack time at school to bath time with extra bubbles. Josh turned to me. "Mama?" he asked, waiting for my answer.

I wondered if it was appropriate to share my response out loud. "After . . ." I started, but lost courage once the first word escaped my lips. "I mean, I like breakfast time. I like any time of the day that involves good food." And that *was* true—I did like mealtime and snack time and all the times where food was a staple. But what I'd really wanted to say was, *"After bedtime, when all the kids are asleep,"* and I wasn't sure how that might sound to my children, coming from their own mother.

Eleanor turned to Josh. "What about you, Papa?" she asked. He didn't hesitate. He didn't fumble. "Oh, after bedtime of course. When all of you are asleep." His silly delivery of the words made the children laugh as he leaned in their direction. He looked at me with such a bright smile in his eyes, I was reminded all over again why I love him so much. For starters, he's painstakingly honest, and he gets me. He had taken the words right out of my mouth.

I'd always dreamed of having my very own big family. And "a big family" is just another way of saying "loud dinner table." The two go hand in hand. In a way, I'd always dreamed of having my very own loud dinner table. Yet lately, the loud table I once longed for was the last place I wanted to sit down—amid the mess, the noise, the noodle-flying and bum-shaking, with children ignoring any command or empty threat this desperate mama had left to dish like it was some huge serving of stinky, burnt Brussels sprouts.

I often think back to an afternoon when my family was crossing Columbus Avenue on the Upper West Side. It was a sunny Sunday, and we were walking home from church. The kids were flocked neatly around our double stroller in their Sunday best: Eleanor's hair methodically pinned in a crown braid atop her head, the boys in their sharp three-piece blue suits complete with ties and matching dress shoes. I'd even remembered to clip everyone's fingernails before we left the apartment, a feat in and of itself. (We'd only recently graduated from the season of life where I'd clip one child's nails after they were in a deep sleep, headlight attached to my forehead during the endeavor. This took place in the pitch-black cave of their bedroom. Pick your battles, they say.)

As we crossed the street, with no one arguing or bothering or poking one another, you could almost sense a special, happy skip in each kid's step. I was thinking, *My gosh, Naomi—your big family dream has come to fruition, and will you look at it?! It's picture-perfect.*

This moment was interrupted almost instantaneously by an older man passing us while heading the opposite direction. He shouted, "Too many kids!" as we crossed paths.

We hadn't been in his way, hadn't bumped him, hadn't done anything but cross the street, quietly during a rather peaceful moment. Our family hadn't reached the sidewalk on the other side of the street, but I could no longer hold in the laughter. I felt a bit schooled in an odd way. I felt a bit put in my place too. That picture-perfect moment I'd been frolicking through in my head? Yeah, it was over.

This man looked almost identical to that grumpy old man from the Pixar movie *Up*—white hair poking out from under his flat flannel cap and eyes almost entirely hidden behind thick, black-rimmed glasses. And the way that unsolicited opinion rolled off his tongue, like a true born-and-raised New Yorker. I'm well aware that a family of seven walking down a street in Manhattan is often a spectacle. I don't think it should be, but I've heard enough of the whispers when we pass strangers who turn to their companions and gasp things like, "*Look* at all those kids!" and "Did you just see that?" To a lot of people, five kids is too many. And I couldn't suppress my laughter after we passed that sweet old man in the crosswalk, because most days five kids is too many kids for *me*.

Yet five kids is also just right. The five greatest gifts I've been given. The five breathing beings with warm hugs and sticky fingers that have pushed me to know myself more, be better, try harder, love unconditionally, give everything willingly, because they've shown me a world where life really is picture-perfect—even with the breakfast Cheerios mixed in with the dinner noodles on the floor beneath the loud dinner table. It's

This vision of a mess is just right. It's picture-perfect in its own eccentric, colorful way.

rarely a neatly groomed party crossing the street in their Sunday best, and we're always two short steps away from accidents and tears with the commotion that is "too many kids," but this vision of a mess is just right. It's picture-perfect in its own eccentric, colorful way.

And as the kids grow and want their tablets at the table and then graduate to having lives of their own that pull them away from the table entirely, I hope we've nurtured that roaring loudness enough that they'll still want to bring that energy and love to our dinner table. As they become grown adults coming home again with blossoming lives and their own families, please let the dinner table be loud. And in the meantime, please let me embrace this wonder that is mine: the big family, the loud dinner table.

PART FIVE

MOTHER IS A VERB

DATE: july 2019 (with a quick flashback to april 2011)

LOCATION: jackson, wyoming (and hi, target parking lot located in arlington, virginia, 2011!) ←

HAIRSTYLE: the final remnants of my first perm, which felt confusingly controversial online yet i couldn't have loved more

FAVORITE FOOD: if i get to eat it while it's still hot, with no baby on my lap, i don't care. i'm into it!

NUMBER OF LITTLES: it's a party of five kids in this one!

Shoesies

While walking out of our hotel in Jackson, Wyoming, with my five children around me, an employee behind the front desk became excited at the sight of us. "Twins?" she asked. Her voice pitched high as she lifted her hands to her cheeks. Three more strangers flocked around the double stroller, each bending low to gaze sweetly at fourteen-month-old Beatrice and Madalena. We exchanged pleasantries, and my babies responded with their version of high fives.

"I've got twin girls too," one of the women said. "Twenty-one years old now." Her tone was nostalgic as she touched my little ones' feet. "Where are your shoesies? Gosh, your feet must be so cold!" Then she turned back to address me directly, this time with a much harsher tone. "You need some socks and shoes on them!"

I looked down at my baby girls, both strapped safely in their stroller on a warm and sunny July day. Suddenly I was snapped back to a Target parking lot outside Washington, DC, when Eleanor was about the twins' age, maybe a few months younger. She sat happily in her car seat, attached securely on the shopping cart beside me as I loaded the trunk with shopping bags. A swaddle blanket was tucked over her, but her bare feet extended out into the cool late-spring air.

"Mommy, Mommy! Where are my shoes, Mommy?" A woman in her sixties approached my then baby girl and, touching her feet, continued to speak in a sugary voice, as though she were the tiny human birthed from my womb. "Mommy, put some socks on me, Mommy! My feet are cold."

I'd been a young, new mother then, with no close mom friends and all my extended family living several states away. I'd been trying to figure things out, trying to stay positive and upbeat, all while feeling heartbreakingly alone most days. Parenting had often felt overwhelming and tiring, and while constructive criticism is one thing, the new world of motherhood at times felt oh-so-very judgmental.

"You did your car-seat straps wrong." "She shouldn't be touching that." "You shouldn't let your baby crawl on the museum floor." "She needs more tummy time." "She needs less tummy time." "My baby would have been asleep by this time at night."

The criticisms were frequent. And loud. They echoed even louder at times as I publicly blogged and shared bits and pieces of my daily life through pictures and stories. Most of the time the online community felt like my family, but sometimes, unsolicited advice and harsh judgments were unsettling to a newly minted mother. While I loved my new role and lived solely to keep my baby girl happy, healthy, and safe, these negative opinions weren't doing much for my confidence, and in those days I didn't know how to brush them off.

Over time, taking all the external feedback to heart became, well . . . exhausting.

Standing in that Target parking lot, I desperately wanted to feel validated by the stranger. I explained the situation at hand, fearing she might call Child Protective Services on me right then and there. Almost begging, I frantically said things like, "Oh no, look. I have socks right here in my diaper bag. They kept falling off inside the store, so I put them in here so I wouldn't lose them! I have them, see? We're getting into the warm car right now, where I will make sure her car-seat straps are properly secured and I won't even drive if she cries! I'll pull over! I am a good mom! I am a really good mom! See?! The socks you mention, the socks are right here in my diaper bag!" All of it code for "Please know I'm trying. I'm trying my absolute hardest. I don't know a lot of what I'm doing, but I love her more than life itself and I *am* trying." I even teared up as I kept reaching for the woman's approval and understanding.

I eventually got Eleanor strapped into the car before walking around to the driver's seat, where I sat down, shut my car door, and turned on the engine all in one motion. There I sat, gazing at my baby girl in the rearview mirror but not leaving the parking lot for several more minutes. Everything was spinning and it felt like my heart had fallen through my stomach. I'd been gutted by a complete stranger. And it hurt. I felt panic. I felt hot tears. But mostly I felt sad, fearing I wasn't a good mom.

Fast-forward eight years and five kids later, to a hotel lobby in Jackson, Wyoming, where another older stranger offered the same unsolicited claims: "You need some socks and shoes on them!" I looked at this woman, who stared at me condescendingly while still touching my baby girls' feet, and all I could do was smile. It was a genuine smile. Sincere, not a snarky "seriously?!" smile. A real, honest smile. No words surfaced, and for a minute I wondered if I'd just become too tired to explain myself or if I'd finally grown enough in my mothering to not care what this stranger thought. A little bit of both, I think. But more so the latter.

Now when I see a new mother on the street, it takes everything in me not to run up to her and say, "You're doing a great job! You've got this!" Instead, I try to soften my words by offering something along the lines of "Congratulations!" And maybe, if there's time or it feels right, "She's beautiful . . . how are you doing?"

Of course, it would've been easier from the onset if I'd possessed the confidence level I now have in my mothering. Yet I understand that time and experience shape that personal growth. I don't know where another woman might be in her own self-discovery journey, but I do know that I have the gift of offering her a smile, a compliment, a kindness, a helping hand if needed. And I also know we all have that power. We all have that gift, and we should dare to share it.

> I am an imperfect mother, but I have unconditional love for each and every one of my babies.

I didn't have my daughters' socks in my diaper bag in Jackson, Wyoming. I didn't even have their shoes. But I did have confidence in myself and my mothering. I no longer doubted the truth that I am a good mother. Just like *you* are a good mother. I am an imperfect mother who makes mistakes and doesn't have it all figured out, but I have unconditional love for each and every one of my babies. When I have questions, I research and look for answers. Beyond that, my bandwidth has no capacity to give any attention to unsolicited questions, advice, and opinions on my parenting. As we mamas honor ourselves for doing the best we can and smile in response to the criticisms, we rest easy, knowing our unconditional love for our children is more than enough.

DATE: summertime, 2016

LOCATION: soho, new york city

HAIRSTYLE: i gave myself some baby bangs and you can totally tell i did them myself :-

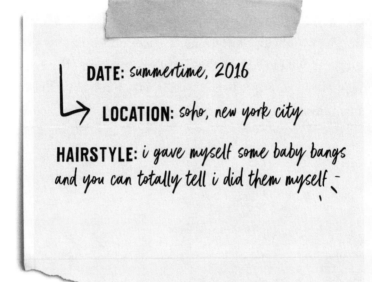

FAVORITE FOOD: yes, the cronut from dominique ansel bakery is amazing, but have you tried his chocolate chip cookie?! mind. blown.

NUMBER OF LITTLES: uno, dos, tres!

Just a Mom

Crowded around the entrance of a low-lit and rather loud restaurant in SoHo, my friends and I greeted one another with hugs and weary smiles. It was late into the evening, as we'd waited for our babies to fall asleep before daring to sneak away for a mom's night out—a rare occurrence only attainable thanks to big magic tricks happening back at our homes.

It took a certain kind of spell to get us all there together without children at our hips, a spell requiring the help of kind partners who'd ushered us out the door after many of them were just arriving home from a long day at their own workplaces. We'd all done our version of mixing the ingredients for a delicate bedtime potion, with the right amount of nursing babies to sleep or reading books to toddlers while rubbing their backs and playing with their hair and encouraging them (sometimes patiently, sometimes less patiently) to go to sleeeeeeep. Then came the grand finale trick of tiptoeing away from where they rested their heads, trying to avoid the creaks in the floor that always seemed to wake them, even though blaring sirens on the busy streets never caused the slightest stir. Magic, I tell you. It takes a special kind of magic to orchestrate a mom's night out.

I'd worn very high heels, which made walking difficult but gave me that feeling of fanciness I often missed when wearing my go-to mama sneakers and flats. Who cares about difficulty walking when you know you'll be eating your meal hot and finishing your sentences without tiny bosses poking and prodding you? I not only braved the high heels; I welcomed them.

While waiting for our table, I bounced in and out of conversations to my left and then my right, shuffling in place in my magical high-heeled shoes. We all talked at lightning speed, determined to catch up before the fairy-tale clock struck midnight and the glamorous night ended.

As we settled in at our table, we took turns introducing ourselves to one girlfriend's good friend, someone new to us who was visiting from out of town. In doing so, the conversation turned to some of the exciting things we had going on in our lives. Many of these women were devoted and loving mothers also producing beautiful work outside of their mothering, sharing their talents with the world in many different ways.

One was a photographer who'd recently shot a big project downtown. Another was in the final stages of launching her second business, and another had her own clothing line that seemed to be growing at a successful rate. One was a nurse part-time and another was working as a personal trainer. I was working on my blog full-time. We'd made our way around the table to the final friend, when the out-of-towner asked her, "And what do you do?"

My good friend, a mom of three children under the age of four at the time, replied, "Oh . . . I'm just a mom."

Just.

Just?

Knowing my sweet friend, I'm sure the question didn't bother

her in the least, and our new out-of-town friend replied warmly as we continued the conversation and moved along. But the words stuck with me, and I kept revisiting her answer in my head as the night carried on.

After we'd said our goodbyes at the uptown subway station and walked our separate ways home, I grew increasingly angry. Partly because of my shoe choice—the high heels were a true pain by that point—but also because that phrase, *just a mom*, still didn't sit well with me.

I started to hear it more and more after that conversation in SoHo—women of all sorts placing the word *just* into their intros when sharing news that they were mothers. As though it wasn't as courageous, as exciting, or as ambitious as choosing to do something else with their lives. As though motherhood wasn't enough, isn't enough, will never be enough.

In this day and age, women are blessed with the ability to find our identities in something outside of being homemakers, mothers, or wives, thanks to the brave work and diligent fight of many warrior-women who came before us and are in our midst even now. We live in a time when we can explore our many talents in countless ways. While all of this is incredible and magnificent and glorious, how did we push mothering so far down the list of powerful job titles that it garners a *just*? Can't we continue to find pride and a sense of accomplishment in our role as mothers too? Even if it's the only job title we claim at a given moment in time? *Especially* if it's the only job title we claim at a given moment in time?

A fire had sparked within me, and the more I heard people say, "just a mother," the more it bothered me. Whenever I heard it, I started asking each woman about that "just." "*Just a mom?!* Just?"

You mean today you *just* washed and folded the laundry of other people, while cooking for them, reading to them, and teaching them, getting down on your hands and knees and playing with them, nurturing and sustaining them, putting many of their needs before yours all day and then all night? You mean you *just* kissed boo-boos and spoke encouraging words and offered unconditional love, while wiping tears and also wiping bottoms? While checking homework and picking up the LEGOs for the sixteenth time that hour? While managing playdates and extracurricular activities and sneaking in their kids' vitamins and also their vegetables and somehow managing to get teeth brushed and make it on time to places while—most importantly—also providing an atmosphere of complete safety and love? You mean you're *just* building up the next generation of kind, motivated, hardworking, and incredible people who will change the world for the better because of the day-to-day, diligent effort you are making to show up at all hours for your precious babies?

What you're doing isn't *just* mothering. It is Mothering. And it is everything. It's hard work; it's exhausting. It's around the clock. Sure, it's messy and mundane at times, devastating and heart-wrenching at other times. It can cause you to feel alone, and it can bring a level of anxiety you've never before known. It may even change your relationship with your body in ways you didn't anticipate. And of course, it'll come with obnoxious demands like requiring the soundtrack to a single animated children's film

> What you're doing isn't just mothering. It is Mothering. And it is everything.

to be played all day every day for far too many days to count. All in all, it's a lot. And it's not for everyone. But I have to tell you: Motherhood is powerful. It can be fulfilling. And it is important. Giving life, nurturing life, raising a human being to be a loving, good, and kind soul in this world . . . what could matter more?

Parenting is a gift and a privilege I hope you or I never downplay. No matter how many job titles you juggle, or if you juggle that one job title alone. You are not *just a mom*. **You are a mother!**

Believe in your importance. Believe in your incredibly beautiful and demanding work. Omit the *just* in front of your title next time you introduce yourself and say, "I am a mother" confidently, with conviction and pride. Because the work you do is valuable and crucial and respected. And you are too.

DATE: spring 2013 (and a brief nod to a spring a few seasons earlier, in 2011)

LOCATION: a park bench in front of the flatiron building, with a scene at a burger joint in dc a few years earlier

HAIRSTYLE: long, long, long! and through both stories, no bangs!

FAVORITE FOOD: pistachio gelato, where have you been all my life?

NUMBER OF LITTLES: a one-year-old samson, a two-year-old eleanor (and a scene in dc with a four-month-old eleanor! sorry, is this confusing yet?!)

You Can Feed Her Anywhere . . .

I sat beside my friend on the park bench, each of us bouncing our second babies on our laps, both of whom were roughly at the one-year-old mark. We were playing a massive game of catch-up, since my friend and her husband lived all the way in Arizona, and we hadn't seen them for a few years. Our husbands stood together in the distance, chatting and holding our spot in the long, winding line toward burgers and fries at the original Shake Shack stand in Madison Square Park. Spring was in full bloom, with birds chirping loudly and blossoms peeping out of the bushes behind our bench, their floral scent permeating the air around us. Our older children were tucked beside our feet, with a bucket of sidewalk chalk and some bubbles to keep them occupied.

"Naomi, look at you!" my friend commented, gesturing with one arm toward me and baby Samson, whom I had begun to nurse as we sat together.

"What?" I responded, looking down at my chest, wondering if I had something on my shirt.

"Look at you!" she said again. "This is amazing. I'm so proud of you. . . . Do you remember what this was like the last time I saw you?"

It took me a minute to piece her meaning together. "Oh yeah," I thought out loud, jogging my own memory. As I mentally replayed the moment she referenced, part of me wanted to laugh and another part of me wanted to cry as I experienced the array of emotions that came with reliving the buried memory. "Oh my gosh. I had completely forgotten!"

The last time we'd been together was two spring seasons earlier, in Washington, DC. Eleanor had been about four months old, and she and I had met up with these same out-of-town friends at another burger joint by Josh's office near the White House. I'd spent the majority of our lunch date not with our friends at our table but in a bathroom stall with my baby girl—because it was lunchtime, and Eleanor was hungry.

At the time, I'd believed hiding in a bathroom stall was where I was supposed to be while breastfeeding my baby. "Hey," this same friend had said quietly, catching my eye when I arrived back at the table as the meal was being cleared away. "You can feed her here. You can feed her anywhere." Her tone was gentle but also firm. "You know that, right?" Part of me knew it, but a larger part of me didn't yet know how to lend support and love to that other part of me.

Sitting on closed toilet seats in bathroom stalls all over the DC area, bathrooms discovered while shopping for groceries, running errands, visiting museums, and doing everything else, I awkwardly hunched over my fragile new baby propped on my lap. I'd feed her behind the dirty doors, my tense shoulders lifted and pulled forward, in the hope that my upper body curved around her would offer protection from the unsanitary setting of her meal. And as someone in the stall to my left or right occasionally flushed her toilet, the loud whoosh of water startling Eleanor, I'd adjust her latch on my breast and softly stroke her head and think, *This is so stupidly wrong.* Even so, I stuck with the routine. And each time a feeding needed to happen and we weren't anywhere near our one-bedroom apartment on the Hill, the sweaty, nervous search for a public bathroom that provided a semiprivate setting commenced.

Before all of this, during my third trimester of pregnancy with Eleanor, I listened to a different friend, who was not yet a mother, share a long (and, looking back, rather ridiculous) tangent on breastfeeding. Her entire bit was pretty negative, but when she arrived at the idea of a mother feeding her baby in a public setting, she got animated. "It's. So. Gross." She paused between each word for emphasis. Somehow, her authoritative tone triggered me to make a mental note, believing this must be the status quo. *Okay. Don't ever breastfeed in public, especially in front of another person. Because, apparently, "It's so gross."*

While I kept this information somewhere in the back of my mind, my breastfeeding journey did begin on a positive note. The hospital where my eldest daughter was born provided an encouraging lactation consultant, who shared mounds of wisdom and time with me through a nurturing approach. My body churned a steady milk flow, my husband was thoroughly supportive (sweetly making sure I remained well hydrated and fed at all hours), and Eleanor was a healthy eater (though she never once took a bottle successfully, which meant we were latched together always).

I enjoyed nursing and quickly grew confident in my ability to nourish Eleanor around the clock as I fed on demand. We made quite the team, Eleanor and I, a team that would continue our nursing adventure into and throughout my entire pregnancy with her brother, Samson, and then after his birth, into the tandem stage, nursing the two together (sixteen months apart in age), until I weaned Eleanor at the age of two and a half while continuing on with Samson. While tiring at times, I loved the breastfeeding stage. Acknowledging with respect that the experience is different for everyone and that some aren't able or choose not to breastfeed, for me it has undoubtedly been the favorite part of my mothering experience so far—exclusively breastfeeding my five babies over the years.

Even though this breastfeeding journey had a happily-ever-after ending, the first months felt as if I were slaying dragons: feeding Eleanor in public was nothing short of terrifying. I briefly tried a nursing shawl, but goodness gracious my baby girl hated that thing, often ending our nursing session in a full sweat from the poor ventilation of having something draped over her while she ate. Or she'd pull at it in an attempt to uncover herself. (I mean, I get it—eating under a blanket doesn't appeal to me. Although eating while sitting on a toilet doesn't either. But I digress!)

Feeding in public overwhelmed me at first, partly due to the learning curve of nursing in general—adjusting an eightish-pound body that cannot support itself, while I tried to shift layers of clothing and also not flash my bare chest to the entire world, latching her, knowing when to burp her, and wondering if she was getting hindmilk, all before she screamed. Because her screaming or fussing heightened my stress, and then my milk would suddenly announce itself by leaking sideways and upways and pretty much *all* the ways. Despite these trials during my quest for nursing bliss, the biggest hurdle—as a first-time mom navigating first-time everything—was my fear of offending someone by feeding my baby in their line of sight and being a bother in some way. It pains me to admit that now, but it's taken a lot of intentional mental work to quiet that nonsense.

I don't recall the first time I decided to skip the trip to the bathroom stall and instead feed Eleanor while sitting at the restaurant table. But slowly, with a friend in a faraway state cheering me on through her heartfelt words shared a month or two earlier, over my cold cheeseburger and melted shake near Josh's White House–adjacent office, I stopped worrying about offending someone by feeding my baby out in the open. And news flash: I didn't poll everyone around me each time I fed in public, so I can't say for sure how they felt. However, during my six years of breastfeeding all around the world, no one ever approached me and told me it was gross. No one ever approached me and said anything.

With time, I learned to unclasp my nursing bra and latch on my baby girl with just one hand, ever so discretely. I learned to keep calm and cool during our feedings, even if she screamed or fussed and I felt others' eyes looking over. With practice, breastfeeding became second nature. I especially learned to stop stressing in my own head, wondering if something I was doing over here might be offending someone over there.

As the years have passed and our family has grown, my confidence in doing what I feel is best

I especially learned to stop stressing in my own head, wondering if something I was doing over here might be offending someone over there.

for me and my family has also grown. Sure, I still occasionally overanalyze how someone might react, but not as much. It's taken time—and a lot of practice. But I can't discredit the gentle encouragement from friends and family in those moments when I'm trying to find my way. In midstruggle, to have someone catch my eye and say, "Hey, you can feed her here. You can feed her anywhere," or whatever variation of this phrase I might need to hear. *"I see you. How are you? How can I help you? You're doing great."*

And so it happened. Me with my first baby girl, with my next two babies, with my twins. On sidewalk corners, in crowded airplane rows, leaning over car seats, on the playground, on the beach, at the restaurant table, while simultaneously holding my babies and then toddlers, even while walking down the freaking street, I confidently and proudly nourished my five little ones. It was nothing short of an incredible experience, mainly because I wasn't in my own head anymore, worrying if this was okay. Because I believed in myself and the choices I was making, I knew this was okay. I knew this was not "gross."

I saw my friend from Arizona a few months ago and circled back to this encounter, thanking her for what she gave me and reminiscing on how far we've both come since our early mothering days. We both had a good laugh. "I was a little bit in disbelief!" she recounted as she shared her perspective on the park-bench story. "I mean, you just did it so casually—you weren't even thinking about it." That's what happens when you start to own how you choose to live and have wonderful cheerleaders as friends.

DATE: january 17, 2019

LOCATION: new york city

HAIRSTYLE: short, probably dirty. lots of dry shampoo and always in a beanie

FAVORITE FOOD: nursing two, so eating for three which means anything. but also very oddly fond of those haribo peach gummy candies at the moment.

NUMBER OF LITTLES: mother of five! our baby girls just turned seven months old!

Making the Memories, Now

Standing in the cold, bundled in a black wool jacket, a woman adjusted her pretty maroon scarf and glanced my way. She looked both beautiful and wise, with an intriguing elegance. As I approached her, I thought to myself, *Naomi, if you're not dead from lack of sleep by the time you hit your sixties, please carry yourself like this woman right here. Naomi . . . Are you taking mental notes? . . . Naomi?!*

I'd been up most of the night with my baby girls. At just seven months old, Madalena and Beatrice were in that blessed sweet spot where they'd become little people with *big* personalities. It was also that blessed sweet spot where teething was in full force, and using Mama as a human pacifier all night long was their preferred soothing method. You'd think my husband and I would have figured out all the essential parenting tricks by that point, having done this three times prior. But nope! Twins had thrown everything off, and Josh and I had aged fifteen years in those seven months to prove it.

As I pushed my double stroller along West 85th Street in the woman's direction, I had three of my five little ones—my twin girls and their four-year-old brother, Conrad. We were heading toward our favorite Central Park playground when the woman beamed at me with a warm smile as if we already knew each other.

Seeing her stand quietly under a dark-green awning, I couldn't help but smile back at her bright, happy face. I'd nearly passed her when she said it. "You enjoy making those memories, dear. I know it's a lot of hard work, but enjoy making the memories."

Each word hit me *so hard*. Because attached to the sentiment of "enjoy" was her acknowledgment: *"I get it. I've been there."*

Like any mother, I'd heard some rendition of the line "Enjoy every minute!" countless times. But there was something about the way this woman phrased it, with her empathetic tone that expressed nothing but genuine love for something she evidently held close to her own heart—motherhood.

Parenting encompasses a wild compilation of moments that can become a blur, some so mundane and tiresome they could even be summed up as boring. And let's face it. We aren't obligated to enjoy every part of parenting. Most moments would never be found in your family photo album. But this stranger had spoken of "enjoy" in the same breath as "I know it's hard," followed up with the encouragement to "make memories." She knew things I needed to be reminded of, and she'd offered me that infinite wisdom during a random crossing on the crowded city street.

I replied, "Thank you for that. I'm trying. I really am." Then I continued on to the park and never saw her again.

All these months later, I still can't get her striking image out of my mind. Her confident, straight posture in that beautiful wool coat, her contagious smile, and the way she shared something so heartfelt and almost intimate with someone she didn't even know. Has she any idea how much I have carried this with me? How her advice is shaping the mothering I've done since and, hopefully, the mothering that is yet to come?

Leading up to that interaction, I'd been entrenched in a year of survival mode as a mother, a wife, a woman . . . a human being. My motto for 2018 was simple: "*Survive!*" People, likely sensing my exhaustion, had frequently offered up advice, such as "Don't worry. It gets better" or "It won't be so bad when they're older." Some days I'd wonder if I'd ever make it to that future point when my circumstances would be "better."

After spending the first half of the year pregnant with my two baby girls, in a physical and mental state that felt more challenging than anything I'd ever experienced, I transitioned to navigating the second half of the year as a mother to those two newborns and their three beautiful siblings, ages seven, six, and three.

You can bet I'd learned a lot of survival lessons in 2018. About treading water. About how to keep your eyes open with four hours or less of (interrupted!) sleep. About what matters, what doesn't, what's worth it, what's not. What to let go of and what to hold on to as tight as possible forever and ever.

Not long before my rendezvous with the stranger on West 85th Street, I'd set goals for the coming year. I wanted 2019 to be the year I cut out sugar, kicked my soda addiction to the curb (hi, Diet Coke, you terrible, amazing thing, you), and made a habit of waking early each morning so that by the time the kids began to stir, I'd already have exercised, completed my spiritual study, and prepped for the day. But I only lasted until 3:00 p.m. on January 1 before I ate a cookie, and seventeen days in, all my kids were still up bright and early before their mama (such overachievers, these kids). So there I was, realizing this wasn't my time to set lofty goals after all. (How waking up before my children has not gotten any easier all these years into motherhood is beyond me.) No, 2019 wasn't my year for any of that. On the other hand, it wasn't another year to be spent in survival mode either.

But on this day when I encountered the Sage on the Street, I was still struggling to leave survival stage and find my way back to the land of *enjoying*. I had no idea when I'd see another full night of rest, our apartment tidy and organized, or my body back to prepregnancy shape. I was beginning to wonder if any of those things would ever happen. Yet the graceful woman had helped me realize this chaotic mess I stood in would have memories attached to it, whether perfect or not. There wasn't time to wait to begin enjoying them. The time was now.

So as the weeks came and went, I took the stranger's words to heart. While repeating the same motions again and again— changing one baby's diaper and then changing her sister's, right after I'd swept the kitchen floor for a third time in the same evening and broken up some argument between two or three siblings, only to go back to changing one baby's diaper and then her sister's—I'd hold on to the woman's wise words. *"Enjoy making those memories . . . It's a lot of hard work, but enjoy . . ."* During the 3:00 a.m. feeding followed by the 4:00 a.m. feeding followed by the 4:20 a.m. feeding followed by the "Didn't I just feed you six minutes ago?!" feeding, I'd hold on to her words. *"Enjoy making those memories . . . It's a lot of hard work, but enjoy . . ."*

No, it wasn't all rainbows and sunshine, but the small improvements did feel rather large in time. Through my weary eyes, I saw two baby girls looking up and smiling and cooing at me during their diaper changes. I played more on the floor with my four-year-old, even when I was tired and my baby girls were sleeping and I wanted to check out too. I made games out of sweeping the floor with my children at my feet, and I was calmer while breaking up a sibling situation. One of the bigger things? I laughed. I laughed with my family a lot more than I had in a while. And as I nursed one baby girl in the middle of the night only to flip over and nurse her sister shortly after, I found myself stroking their heads in the dark of the room while they fed, feeling their little hands clasped around my thumb. I listened to their adorable purrs, and I whispered, "Mama loves you."

Enjoy. Enjoy making those memories. It's a lot of hard work, but enjoy.

This has become my new mantra, as I show up for my little ones and as I show up for myself. Not eventually, not after this or that happens, but right now. Acknowledging it's hard and exhausting. Acknowledging it's frustrating and boring at times; messy and tiresome pretty much all the time. But *now* is my time to enjoy making these memories. *Now*, while I'm wearing a milk-stained bra and tripping over LEGOs left and right. *Now*, these memories are mine to enjoy while making them.

These memories are mine to enjoy while making them.

Though I'll never be able to properly thank the beautiful stranger on West 85th Street who shaped so much of what I'm working toward, I'm still holding on to and repeating her words to myself each day. I'm enjoying. And I'm hoping you are too.

DATE: sometime in 2012

LOCATION: the back booth of a café in chelsea

HAIRSTYLE: dark and long with reason to celebrate: my grown-out bangs finally tuck behind my ears!

FAVORITE FOOD: learning that chopped vegetables can be delicious if you pair them with fresh mozzarella

NUMBER OF LITTLES: two!

The Dinner

Am I a bad friend?

It was two-something in the morning and I was wide awake in bed, with a mind that couldn't stop racing as I stared at the darkened ceiling while replaying the scene over and over in my head. The scene had taken place months earlier, at dinner with a friend who'd been one of my closest, our friendship spanning many years. Our relationship had covered a lot of ground, with shared experiences and vulnerable conversations where few topics felt off the table. She challenged me intellectually as she'd talk about God or politics, while also never being above discussing crappy reality TV and all the conspiracy theories and spoilers that come with it. (I mean, *The Bachelor* is a great television show—don't let Josh Davis tell you otherwise.) The bottom line is we had fun together. So much fun.

But that dinner was a turning point. While the two of us sat at our table, I felt like I was up on the ceiling watching the entire scene from a different angle, and this perspective provided me a new insight to digest along with the meal. When our check arrived about fifty minutes later, I realized I'd said a total of maybe three sentences all evening. My friend had so many stories she wanted to get off her chest, and I wanted to be a good friend and listen. As our dishes were cleared away, I realized something that brought new meaning to our friendship and was rather devastating to comprehend in real time. She wasn't recounting these stories for advice or input or even to vent or get support or encouragement. She hadn't asked me a single question about my thoughts on any of her stories, let alone a single question about me and my life. I was only her audience.

As we stood to put on our coats before leaving the restaurant, she asked in a way that felt like an afterthought: "How about you? Things are good?"

Well actually, no. I'd had a long week with my kids and was also in the final rounds of a big creative collaboration that felt both exciting and stressful. I had color swatches I wanted her feedback on and a funny story to share too. But now, taken aback by what transpired during the last hour, I had my guard up. I wasn't going to share any of this. Because I realized she didn't really care.

I'm sure she cared, at least a little. However, the current scenario now begged for our relationship to be looked at through a different lens. I replayed past conversations with my friend. They confirmed a lot of what this current dinner outing had revealed. Our friendship wasn't exactly the healthiest, and while it was a lot of fun at times, it was lopsided in many ways.

At that stage in my life, I was slowly realizing how much of a people pleaser I'd always been. And the thought of offending or disappointing anyone in my circle made my stomach drop. I often catered to my friends and their asks and needs and wants, and I happily did so, because I like my friends and I like helping.

I feel flattered and humbled to drop everything when they need a listening ear, or someone to watch their kids for a few hours when a sitter falls through (and that they trust me to do this), or someone to lend support and love whenever and however, no questions asked, because that's what friends do. Friends often do these kinds of things for me, too, and I'm so thankful. I believe supporting and cheering them on, without concern for reciprocation, is what friendship is all about. So while it's not about counting favors or having a "What's in it for me?" mentality, I was beginning to comprehend a pattern of *take-take-take* in this particular relationship that didn't feel great. It didn't feel like friendship.

A few weeks after our dinner, I called my friend to share a bit of how I was feeling. She remained disinterested, with her long pauses and requests to repeat myself that suggested she was multitasking on the other end of our call. As time moved forward, with the significant milestone of a work collaboration and my birthday, I hadn't heard from my friend. I didn't think much of it. I'm the worst at remembering birthdays, and I understand how much each woman I know juggles. But the pattern was growing apparent: my friend only entered my life when it was convenient for her or when she needed something.

Several months later, she texted me. When I first saw her name pop up on my phone, I was excited. As I read her message, I was bummed. She wanted my help promoting something on my blog and social media channels. After putting my kids to bed, I spent what felt like forever drafting and deleting more than a dozen replies. (Hi, people pleaser.) Some were super lengthy, as I tried to explain how I felt and where I was coming from. In the end I kept it short and simple, saying I was sorry, but I wouldn't be able to do the promotion she requested right now.

She didn't reply. We didn't talk again.

I knew it was for the best, but it made me feel like a bad friend, and I didn't like that. We *had* had so much fun together over the years. And I believed her to be a good person, which made me wonder if I should get over it, share her thing, and let it go—and perhaps continue to meet up for one-sided conversations over meals. As I rehashed small details from our last few interactions, I considered reaching out and being like, *"Sorry! Don't hate me—let me share the project you need me to share. Please don't be mad!"*

As time ticked on, and I invested and gave and supported in friendships where I felt we equally loved and lifted each other, the worrisome feelings of being a bad friend to my former friend faded. While some relationships can improve as both people show up and do the work, I knew deep down that this particular relationship wasn't balanced.

When evaluating friendships, I've learned to ask myself questions you can also ask: How do I feel walking away after conversations with friends? Do I feel uplifted, encouraged, and inspired? Do I feel heard, even when we disagree? Do I believe I have to fit a certain mold when I'm around those friends, or do they believe they need to fit a particular mold around me? Is negativity involved, through gossiping or complaining or focusing on things that don't matter? At the end of the day, do our friendships make us feel nourished and loved and provide opportunities to nourish and love them back?

As my road into motherhood has expanded fivefold, my time and capacity for female friendships have diminished—even though it takes a freaking village (or city) of warrior women to navigate this chapter of life. In addition to asking myself the questions above, this is yet another driver for examining friendships, revising them at times, and ending them entirely on occasion, since there's no room for fluff friendships when you're in the thick of life.

While working through this friend anxiety, I found new confidence in fiercely protecting my small circle of close friends, and I didn't worry so much about pleasing all the others. My early thirties taught me that sometimes friendships don't end with a dramatic falling out. Two friends can grow and change in different directions and lose connection, commonalities, and interests. Friend breakups (for lack of better phrasing) are natural, as seasons of life take us on diverging journeys and we need to say goodbye. This doesn't make you a bad friend, and it doesn't make the other person a bad friend either.

> *Friend breakups (for lack of better phrasing) are natural, as seasons of life take us on diverging journeys and we need to say goodbye.*

I am not a bad friend.

I am an imperfect friend, but a good friend. I show up for and invest in my people, as they do for me. And when hurdles or frustrations or disappointments arise, as happens in relationships, we work it out as respectful adults who are trying our best. If a friendship shows its true colors as unhealthy and one-sided, it doesn't make you a bad friend to let it go, safeguard yourself and your village, and move on.

DATE: can anyone smell that "bouquet of newly sharpened pencils"?! (i watch you've got mail every autumn) school is now in session, fall 2019

LOCATION: the elementary school playground on the upper west side

→ **HAIRSTYLE:** all i know is it's still hot outside but i don't care i've busted out my beanies

FAVORITE FOOD: i have a milk duds stash in my desk drawer and none of my children have found it yet ———

NUMBER OF LITTLES: five, but conrad just started kindergarten (i'm not ugly crying!) so i'm missing my oldest three during much of the day . . .

Hello, Friend

"It's not a big deal . . ." Her voice trailed off as she tried to brave the tears that were slowly catching in her lower eyelashes. "Can we just go?" She looked around the crowded playground where we stood, just minutes after elementary school dismissal, while my heart sank. I pulled her in for a big, tight hug and blinked back the tears welling up above my own lower eyelashes.

I knew this day would come eventually. I just didn't anticipate how early it would arrive—smack-dab one month into third grade. What the freaking heck?! My firstborn daughter, my sweet eight-year-old who doesn't have a mean bone in her body, experiencing her first encounter with a group of girls who weren't very kind. A group of girls who declared on this day, in front of Eleanor, that they didn't want her to play with them anymore. She was confused and crushed. The mama bear in me wanted to light the playground on fire and give each of them a piece of my mind in my most thunderous, screeching yell. But I knew nothing gets solved that way, and Eleanor was my main focus. Besides, I didn't have any matches.

"You know what we need?" I held on to her as we finished

our hug. "A mama-daughter date, right now! That's what we need. Let's go."

After making quick arrangements with Josh for a tag-team swap with our other children, Eleanor and I made our way from the playground gates toward our favorite bakery around the corner. I squeezed her hand at the crosswalk as she shared how she didn't get it, she didn't understand. I wanted to be able to tell her it gets better, but I knew, from my own life experiences as a woman, that it doesn't necessarily get better. "I know, Eleanor. I'm so sorry. I don't understand it either."

I understand it a bit. I'm bothered by it a lot.

A few of my friendships as an adult woman have felt unnecessarily complicated. I own up to the fact that on occasion, I contribute to the complications by bringing my array of trust issues to the table, by way of a high emotional guard that doesn't budge without proper time and care. Also, living in one of the most transient cities in the world during my twenties and early thirties has meant meaningful and vulnerable friendships are just taking shape when friends unexpectedly say goodbye, when new zip codes summon them, when work or school or family ties demand their presence. It's a strange cycle I truly resent.

And while I feel grateful for technology offering a kind hand in making the separation less painful, via texts and emails and (FaceTime or Marco Polo) video chats, despite our best efforts, the lack of daily face-to-face interaction presents challenges. As time passes, the strength that often builds a female bond from physical interaction eventually diminishes, making the friendships less resilient. Of course, it's possible to maintain deep relationships with women outside one's neighborhood confines, but as with all long-distance relationships, it's not the easiest. And then there's the fact that the responsibilities of adulthood thin our free minutes, and some friendships fall to the wayside as life carries us down different pathways (see "The Dinner" chapter).

These circumstances keep me in a permanent state of appreciation for the handful of close friendships I hold dear and work to cultivate further. When I think about why *those* friends, it's because I've come to know what quality women they are, to their core. And when I think about why I'm drawn to them and value them so highly, it's because I leave their presence feeling better. I feel motivated, uplifted, inspired, appreciated, supported, heard, forgiven, respected, and loved for being me.

This is a harsh contrast to other friendships when I've left feeling anything but, because our bond was built on other, less positive things that may bring women together—the webbing of gossip, engrossing stories at another's expense, and an overall pessimistic approach. While I've tried to steer clear of these associations since my elementary school days, I admit I've been culpable at times. I'm not proud of it.

Being a mother of three daughters, who will undoubtedly experience a fair amount of heartache at one point or another in their friendships, has brought a magnifying lens on my private interactions with female friends. It's tragic to witness how quickly a jab can be shared without intentional malice.

"Yeah, she's pretty, but I heard her hair is really thin." "Did you notice she isn't wearing her wedding ring?" "I feel like she's dressing differently now. I hope she's doing okay."

I'll replay the conversation in my head and think, *How did that even come up?!* A quick traverse over my lifetime, spanning countless conversations with girlfriends, displays several memories that prick as I recall being the one who shared a story that wasn't mine to share, who speculated on a falsehood, lamented about someone to cover an insecurity or jealousy or hole in my life that I believed would be filled, fixed, or fastened by putting someone else down. And as I recall being the one to share a story to make myself feel better about something, the prick is forever solidified by the confirmation that sharing never made me feel better about anything.

Having been on the opposite side of this play too—where I've felt the devastating sting of rumors, exaggerated stories, and falsified opinions from brief interactions with others who later asserted themselves as authoritative figures on my personal life—I'll tell you right now: it's not worth it. If a girlfriend speaks poorly of someone you both know, chances are high she speaks poorly of *you* when you're not around. I learned the painstakingly hard way that no one is off limits when someone can't rein in their obsession of commanding a room at another's expense. I've finally seen through it, and I want no part of it.

None of us are perfect, but we all should be wanting to check ourselves and our friends, and do better. We can surround ourselves with women who always speak kindly of others, always, and we can be the ones to change the topic if unkind whispers begin to take shape.

I can't shield my daughters from the distress they'll likely encounter in friendships as their lives move forward. I won't always be there to whisk them away for a mama-daughter cookie date when the going gets tough. But I want them to know that while friendships will at times be confusing and maddening and heartwrenching, they can choose how they approach every interaction with others. And I'm determined to fill each of their toolboxes with everything they need to navigate the more complicated areas of friendships—to be the girls, and later the women, others gravitate to because of their kindness, their supportive words, their countenance exuding love.

While I'll work tirelessly to fill each daughter's toolbox, the best way I'll fill it is by my own example. By putting myself in check each day when interacting with friends and others. And during the times I think I'm off duty as Mama—such as when I'm all alone on the phone with a friend—because their little ears and minds and hearts are being conditioned more so in these moments than others. As women we have such power and pull on the younger generation of girls, whether our daughters or others. I have a hunch that when we nurture those kind, spongelike spirits with which our daughters come to earth—by being mindful of how we speak of, converse with, and interact with other women—we might make a lot of headway, including for the girls on the playground in third grade who are learning power plays and unkind mannerisms from somewhere. In doing so, the roots of our own female friendships will strengthen and deepen, as our words and actions blossom into something better when we're together.

> *As women we have such power and pull on the younger generation of girls, whether our daughters or others.*

PART SEVEN

FAMILY FIRST

DATE: spring 2007

LOCATION: larry's office ←

HAIRSTYLE: shoulder length and no bangs and always pulled up thanks to that dancer life

FAVORITE FOOD: constantly craving the curry from penang and the chocolate souffle from café mozart. rest in peace to both incredible places that are no longer

NUMBER OF LITTLES: talking lots about a future family, but this is before any of those darlings came along . . .

She's Getting Married

With my legs configured into a pretzel on the floor outside the dance studio, I was midstretch, waiting for my next three-hour rehearsal period to begin, when the dance department secretary slipped me the note: *Larry would like to see you in his office.* I felt sick before I even finished reading the sentence. Larry, the artistic director of the Dance Division at the Juilliard School, where I was in my third year, wasn't my favorite person in the world. He'd tell you without hesitating that I wasn't exactly his either. Larry was an incredible teacher with a gift for improving anyone's classical technique in a span of one lesson, and I loved beginning my day with his ballet class. He never lingered long on the barre routine and understood the beauty of just getting to the center of the room and *dancing*. However, I respectfully disagreed with many ways in which he ran the dance department.

His office door was already open as I approached. "Come in, come in . . ." He beckoned as he sat down behind his desk. I don't recall exchanging any pleasantries before he got right to the point: "I heard your news." He motioned to my hand, where a diamond engagement ring now resided. Josh had asked me to marry him a few weeks earlier.

"Oh right, yes . . ." My right hand immediately clasped my left, hiding my ring. I'd anticipated a conversation around one of his usual critiques—about my body, my being too focused on my love for modern dance and not on my talent for ballet, or something far darker and scarier (but somehow not as nerve-racking) than the direction this conversation was heading.

"What does this mean? Will you be leaving school?" he continued.

I was taken aback and confused. Not that I was expecting a hug from Larry, or even a pat on my shoulder. But as the simple word *congratulations* was missing from his last sentence, I grew defensive as I realized I needed to justify a decision in my private life.

It was something I seemed to be doing a lot lately. Not twenty-four hours after Josh had knelt down on one knee, one of the dearest people in my life reprimanded me as we sat for several hours in my darkened apartment, crying together. "You are throwing your life away. All your hard work, all those hours in the studio. You are too young for this, and it makes zero sense. You are throwing your life away." I knew her words came from a place of love and concern, but they still chipped away at my excitement. Not having my joy shared and acknowledged hurt.

I answered Larry's questions, "Well, no. I'm just getting married. That's all. I'll be married during my senior year—that's all it means." I didn't love the way I phrased my response, but I was busy playing catch-up in my mind as to why this was being turned into a thing.

The next morning before class began, I rehashed the strange interaction with my closest friends. "He probably just thinks if you're getting married, you want to go be a housewife and start having babies," someone suggested lightheartedly. And that made sense from an old-school generational standpoint and because of the emphasis I placed on my faith, which strongly supports family first.

Larry was my department director, which meant he'd invested a lot in me and my future as one of only twelve women from around the world admitted to the program each year. I could understand why he wanted confirmation that my marriage wouldn't interfere with my time at Juilliard. Also, I was twenty years old. I understood then, as I do now, that marrying at that age can seem super bizarre to many. Perhaps I felt defensive for an array of reasons.

Someone in the Office of Student Affairs later told me that to date, I was the only member of the dance department to get engaged and then marry while receiving my bachelor of fine arts degree. Even if getting married during college might be normal elsewhere, it had never happened in the Dance Division of the Juilliard School.

(An interesting side note I'm pleased to report: the dance department at Juilliard has since seen several more married students and even a few pregnancies, while the soon-to-be mamas multitasked and completed their degrees. While I wasn't there when these marriages and pregnancies took place, I was overjoyed to learn the atmosphere at the school, with a new female dance director, was welcoming and supportive of women.)

Life in the dance studio aside, I encountered surprising reactions to my new life decision outside my college campus too. A few weeks after getting engaged, I wandered into a nail salon. With the amount of time my left hand felt on display these days, I wondered if some fancy nail polish could distract from the nail-biting habit I'd lived with since childhood. Maybe some fancy nail polish could also distract from the fact that this engagement ring appeared uncomfortable and confusing for a lot of people I knew.

I placed my hands across the table, palms down. Seeing my ring, the manicurist enthusiastically commented, "You're engaged?!" I smiled and nodded. She began shouting in a foreign language to a few of her colleagues at nearby tables, and within a matter of seconds, four women surrounded her, leaning in toward my hands as their eyes panned between my face and the engagement ring. They continued to speak with one another in a different language. I didn't understand what they were saying about me. I felt hot. It was only a few seconds, but everything felt as if it was moving at sloth speed. "How old are you? You are a baby! What is your age?" one of the women asked in English.

In a moment that wasn't my proudest, my twenty-year-old self blurted out a straight-up lie. "I'm twenty-six!" I said, before adding, "I'm *old*!" I'm pretty sure none of them believed me.

Afterward I stood alone on the subway platform and picked at my nails while waiting for the B or C train to take me back to my apartment in Harlem. By the time I reached my front door, my fresh manicure was nearly destroyed because I'd scraped off most of the polish. The fancy polish didn't seem to matter anymore. Instead, I was trying to understand why I felt confident about my decision to marry Josh, yet a bit embarrassed and rather defensive about getting married so young.

It was easy to fall for Josh. He made life special. (Still does, but this story focuses on these early years of dating and engagement.) When I was around him, he had this way of gently removing all the pressures from my outside world, giving me the floor to just be *me*—and figure out who *me* was without interjecting or implying or telling. I loved how much we laughed together as we explored the city late at night after classes and rehearsals ended, as much as we laughed when we sat on the sofa not doing much of anything.

Josh had such great taste in music, books, and style. He also had unrelenting curiosity, which meant he was always reading or learning about something new. He was finishing his degree in economics at Columbia but still made time to take a Martha Graham dance class as one of his courses, to better understand my world. He had this thing for popped collars (still does!). When we discussed our hopes and dreams, shared our thoughts on faith, and revealed goals for the future, so much of what we longed for individually and what we envisioned for a someday family were aligned.

As we fell in love, this was terrifying for both of us to acknowledge, because admitting this meant a substantial shift in our current life trajectories. He was beginning to interview for finance and banking jobs that could take him away from the city and out of the country, and I had a year left of school and was preparing for auditions with dance companies around the US and Europe, including jobs with companies that would undoubtedly tour regularly. But when you know, you know, and who's to say that combining two exciting routes and exploring them together couldn't be something special?

The weight of caring so much about what everyone else thought about me getting married young dragged down on our engagement. I wanted to be confident and cool about the decisions

I was making, but I also wanted others to approve and agree with my choices. Only time and experience would teach me to let go of perceptions and opinions I can't control or change and instead focus on making my life what I want it to be. With time, I've also learned the valuable lesson that I can acknowledge someone's differing opinion while also disallowing it from having a handle on me. I don't need to fixate on it.

I love what Josh says, time and time again, when I start to worry about someone else's opinion on my life choices. He'll shake his head and simply say, "Who cares?!" And that's just it: it's good to care, but that's the wrong thing to care about.

Marrying young (plus an array of other experiences, many of which are documented in this book) has shown me that I don't have to be defensive about living the life I choose to live. It's not always easy to remember, especially when people I greatly care about want a different path for me and voice their frustration or confusion in an unproductive manner.

> *Only time and experience would teach me to let go of perceptions and opinions I can't control or change and instead focus on making my life what I want it to be.*

Out of all the choices I've made in life, choosing to marry Josh remains the best decision. As we've united and built a bond and family, sharing over a dozen years together so far, our partnership has at times shown flaws and challenges. But it's been full of such honest love and laughter from the get-go, something I identified at age twenty and knew I wanted in my everyday future. I'm thankful for it. And for the growth and self-learning marrying under these circumstances taught me.

DATE: february 2014

LOCATION: an all-glass skyscraper in midtown manhattan

HAIRSTYLE: platinum blonde, baby! and fried just a little bit on top

FAVORITE FOOD: fresh pita and hummus, please!

NUMBER OF LITTLES: eleanor is three and samson is not yet two, though he's almost her size!

Let's Do This!

I held Eleanor's and Samson's tiny hands while we stood together just inside the big revolving doors of the all-glass Bank of America tower in Midtown Manhattan. The skyscraper was adjacent to Bryant Park, where we often rode the carousel together and played on the famous steps where the New York Public Library lions lived. But that day's itinerary didn't include carousel rides or library lions, though in a way, it felt every bit as magical. The three of us had our eyes on the tall escalator past the security turnstiles, where we waited patiently for Josh, their papa, to appear at the top of the moving staircase of the building where he had worked each day on the thirty-fourth floor before making his way home to us.

I was nervous and overjoyed and pumped and slightly edgy within the same moment. Josh eventually came into view and waved with both hands in our direction, looking handsome and sharp in his dark suit and tie and wearing the sunniest smile on his face as he passed security and walked toward us. With the back of my hand, I caught a number of happy tears falling down my cheeks as I smiled back. Once across the lobby he knelt, scooped both children into his arms, and brought me in for a hug.

"All right!" he said as we stood together in a tight squeeze. "Let's do this!"

This meant a lot of things, but it mainly signaled the start of our next chapter in life and work and family. The escalator ride to the lobby was Josh's last. He had resigned from working at the bank and was saying goodbye to the corporate world for the time being, to work full-time alongside me. Self-employed, officially! We both felt a lot of emotions on that day, but for the most part, as we huddled and hugged with our kids cozied between us, we felt incredibly grateful—for this chance, for this next phase of life.

Finally getting to a place where we both felt confident in our decision to leave behind Josh's stable and well-paying job—with its health insurance and retirement perks and other cushy benefits—had taken so much work, effort, time, and discussion. We didn't want to take too big a risk, but we also recognized we both thrived on taking risks. Being fully self-employed was new territory for us, but working together wasn't. While I'd started the blog and all the side projects it presented on my own six years earlier, Josh had already been helping me run the business side of *Love Taza* for a few years, in addition to sometimes supporting the creative side (always with official permission from his full-time employers).

The decision to throw ourselves full-time into our entrepreneurial endeavors together felt more right than it did risky. We both loved the creativity our self-employed work challenged us to explore. And calling our own shots—especially making our own decisions and the opportunity to prioritize family—topped the cake, because the flexibility this route provided us to fit our work life into our family life (and not the other way around) is something I'll never take for granted. That alone was what pushed us most to pursue this path.

Growing up, I was a bunhead who believed my only road forward in life was that of being a dancer. My parents graciously poured their finances into classes and programs focused on the art form, and by the time I graduated college with a bachelor of fine arts in dance from Juilliard, which honed my craft to a T, it was a no-brainer that my trajectory as a dancer was forever solidified, jazz hands and all.

And there wasn't anything wrong with that, except for the startling burnout that asserted itself smack-dab in the middle of my college years and grew stifling as I neared graduation. After acknowledging this, it felt slightly rebellious but also strangely gratifying to seek out ways to ignite my love for creativity once again, this time beyond the dance studio. Along with blogging for fun and taking my Polaroid camera with me everywhere, I dabbled in a few styling projects, opened an Etsy shop where I sold handmade hair accessories, and started experimenting with and practicing photography more seriously.

At that time I didn't anticipate how my love for storytelling through personal and random anecdotes, photographs, and videos—along with all the travel tips and hunts for the best burgers and ice cream around my neighborhood and beyond—would one day provide freedom, fun, and financial stability for my growing family, as well as rekindle my love of creating.

And in a way, creating a life I love. Don't get me wrong—at some point, this path became a grounded choice that requires deliberate focus and hours and hours of work. It often meant toiling well into the wee hours of the morning as a new mama wanting to prioritize everything all at once: the nurturing of my kids, the entrepreneurial drive to create, and the goal of loving what I do every day.

It was such a pivotal moment to have my husband, who had always believed in and supported what I'd built so far, ride down that escalator in his suit and tie one last time. To take on the risk as a team member, where together we would stretch ourselves, learn and relearn, make mistakes, and try and fail and try again, but do it together—with the motto and intention to prioritize our family. It's always felt a little bit "pinch me" in a way.

That's not to say working for ourselves in a fast-changing industry, as freelancers with short-term contracts while growing our family to five little ones, hasn't had its share of hurdles. We've been overly ambitious at times. We've failed at things, like an app we built together and a few collaborations we've tirelessly worked on that never came to full fruition in the final hour. We've argued over silly things, like the missing card reader for the camera and redlines in contracts. We both possess strong convictions and specific visions about what's best in many aspects of what we do, and it's been hard at times to share the workload when we've both felt the only way something will get done well is when we interject, overstep, or do it ourselves.

But these six years of full self-employment have reminded me again and again how grateful I am that we took the risk and had the chance to do something together that often doesn't feel like work. Sometimes seeking out what you love and making it yours might be a bit different from the norm, or divergent from what you were told to do or were educated to do or think you should do. Carving your own path is full of risk, but sometimes risk leads to unparalleled rewards. And at the root of it all is believing you can do it. *It* being something you never thought you could do or didn't know existed until last year or still aren't even sure exists, because it doesn't yet. It will take focused effort and arduous work and loads of time; it will take a supportive spouse or friend; and it might even take blood, sweat, and tears. But don't ever let that deter you—believe in your dreams and put in the work and keep pushing for whatever you envision.

We are fortunate to be living in a day and age where we can make our paths truly ours. Thanks to technology especially, if we want to pursue a new hobby or talent, endless resources are available that once could be hard to find. I can't even count how many times I've done a web search where I asked questions like "What does this button on my camera do?" or watched video tutorials online as I've taught myself editing programs for photos, videos, and graphics, like Adobe Lightroom, Final Cut Pro, and Adobe Illustrator. We have information readily accessible to help answer our questions, connect with collaborators, steer us in new directions, and allow us to go after what we want to create, change, and do to better ourselves, our surroundings, and our world.

I think back to that moment in Josh's work lobby, seeing his optimistic smile, seeing him in his suit and tie, and I feel a lot of things. I'm grateful we went for it, for the flexibility and time it granted our family life in the early years of child-rearing. I'm

> Carving your own path is full of risk, but sometimes risk leads to unparalleled rewards.

grateful that we were able to tag-team the workload and child-load and both feel present for such a fast-moving season of life with littles. As the world around us changes and evolves, I imagine our work will do the same, and who knows where it will lead or take us? No matter what, I'll always look back fondly on this chapter we got to spend together, for both the professional and personal accomplishments.

"Let's do this!" Josh had said. And we did. We really did!

DATE: september 2018

LOCATION: my home office, by way of the bathroom tub in our apartment since it's the only room with a working lock on the door . . .

HAIRSTYLE: the postpartum baby hairs are growing back at my higher hairline, which is wonderful news!

though much of the remaining hair on top of my head seems to fall out in clumps these days. you couldn't have shown up at a better time, winter-hat-wearing season!

FAVORITE FOOD: time to bust out the crock-pot: homemade chili season is here!

NUMBER OF LITTLES: cinque!

Tally-Keeping to Tag-Teaming

I found myself stewing in frustration for most of the day. I wanted him to match my level of nerves and stress and exhaustion with some outward display that signaled he felt the same pressures and demands, the same weight and responsibility, among the many other emotions I was experiencing. Yet he was just so chill; he was just so calm.

Meet my husband, Josh. My spouse of over a dozen years, business partner for the past six, and co-parent to our five rambunctious littles. The guy has a legit talent for remaining composed and cool in the most stressful of times, and while that's something I should admire and work to emulate, many times over the years I have instead categorized it as not caring as much as I care. Because in those moments when we're hardly staying afloat, when we've taken on several—maybe too many—work projects that keep piling up (and have just missed a deadline for our biggest brand partnership to date), when we're prioritizing the care and attention we want to give our children while choosing (for better or worse) to have limited outside help for work and childcare (I couldn't speak coherently in the second week of this month from sleep deprivation), shouldn't he be freaking out as much as I'm freaking out?!

The short answer is a resounding no. But the long answer is that this has been a recurring argument for us over the years, as we coordinate family and work responsibilities together while approaching things differently. Sometimes we'll argue about the smallest and silliest things—because we disagree over how to do something, because our roles overlap through the day, because we both have a clear vision for a work project, because someone forgot (probably him), because one of us is hungry (probably me). And while we've always been on the same page with our shared priorities, goals, and work ethic, at times it's been difficult to maneuver through complex days when I've felt strain and stress from all we juggle and believed I was alone in carrying it.

I haven't carried any of it alone, ever. It's been a process, learning to balance differing communication styles, understanding that we manage stress and fatigue in contrasting ways, and trusting each other to show up and do the work, even when we approach tasks in a mismatched manner.

As Josh and I work to cultivate our marriage—on top of working from home while running our small business and managing our family roles and other outside commitments—in a short number of years we've spent more hours together than usual. This has given us ample opportunities to practice identifying the friction and deliberately refocusing our intentions to improve and deepen our relationship. I now recognize when my frustrations are beginning to boil over and can calm myself down to a simmer.

It helps when we sit down frequently to analyze our interactions to better propel ourselves and our relationship forward in a positive direction. Making a conscious effort to be better and do better as individuals and as a team. We return time and time again to five critical ideas that help strengthen our work life, our relationship, and our parenting efforts. Whether you work with your spouse or have kids you raise together, on any average day these ideas all come into play and are universal for bettering any relationship.

The first idea is *a shared, overarching mission to guide you, and common goals to achieve together.* When tensions escalate as I'm pulled in various directions that demand proper time, care, and attention, life can feel overwhelming, as if it's impossible to keep going. I often freeze up and feel practically paralyzed with sheer panic when my to-do list reads as impossible, when the work project looks unfeasible, when the responsibilities and expectations of family life are daunting. Josh and I try our best to recenter ourselves with the shared belief in *family first, work second,* and when we're on the same page with our priorities, everything finds its place under the umbrella of our shared mission.

Second, having *a lack of ego* is important. Josh and I have prioritized being team players and celebrated our successes together. We've understood the need to step up and complete the task, whether the more compelling work, such as creating and writing and one-on-one dates with the kids, or the mundane, everyday jobs, such as the administrative and operational chores, the dishes and trash removal, the diaper duty. When we both simply jump in, irrespective of gender roles or who gets credit, our household thrives, and we're all winning.

The third idea, *hard work,* is important too. Trusting that your partner is working hard, even when you think the workload is uneven (and sometimes it is uneven), is also key. This is where Josh and I have found that being communicative, reporting

When we both simply jump in, irrespective of gender roles or who gets credit, our household thrives, and we're all winning.

back at times, and having confidence that the other partner is doing their best remains paramount. This feels like one of the easiest traps to fall into in relationships: keeping tallies of all the things you've done and comparing it to all the things your spouse hasn't done. Maybe it's just me (I really hope it isn't just me) who's struggled with this. But as I prioritize doing my tasks and trust Josh to do his, as we both also acknowledge and call out each other's strengths in appreciation for what each of us does, the hard work gets done. Plus we're able to recognize and respect so much of what the other one has done, is doing, and continues doing—often behind the scenes.

This is when the fourth idea, *tolerance and forgiveness*, comes into focus. Because we're human, because we're navigating a career path we're carving out as we go, and because each day looks different from the next. Tolerance is the minimum; we aren't simply putting up with each other and ignoring the areas where improvement is needed. Instead, we're striving for a loving atmosphere in all we do, reconciling as we reach for a deeper understanding of each other. This approach increases empathy and drives forgiveness. As I have concentrated on Josh's feelings and he has paid attention to mine, we do what we can to understand where the other person is coming from, and how they approach the tough things like their own frustrations, anger, disappointments, or self-doubt. This exercise makes it easier to not be at each other's throats as we spend thousands of hours together year after year.

And of course, the fifth idea of *celebrating successes and prioritizing having fun together* goes a long way, even when everything else on our plate feels dominant. It's easy to procrastinate sharing physical affection with your spouse, whether you work from home together or not. But that affection has united us as we've prioritized it. There might not be a proper morning send-off by way of a kiss goodbye as one of us heads out the door, or the grand gesture "Honey, I'm home!" in the later evening, as the sound of the proverbial briefcase, purse, or tool bag hits the floor beside the front door, and you embrace and greet each other again. Working from home has encouraged us to discover and create new greetings and rituals in our routines, to emphasize and foster our marriage relationship.

Working together from home isn't for everyone. I understand and appreciate the uniqueness of our setup for the past six years, how at times it has magnified quirks and weaknesses, as we irk each other and press *all* the buttons and I can't seem to find my simmer setting. But spending this much time growing closer— tag-teaming our assignments, sharing in the work we love, and making the effort to put family first—is a cherished gift through and through.

PART EIGHT

FAITH IS LIKE A LITTLE SEED

DATE: a few days before christmas 2016

→ **LOCATION:** new york city

HAIRSTYLE: short, leftover ombre on the ends, debating every single day to cut it or leave it

FAVORITE FOOD: only way to do christmas in the city is with a new treat in hand every four blocks, ideally a levain cookie followed by pain au chocolat from orwashers

NUMBER OF LITTLES: three, but dreaming of a fourth!

The Cop-Out Phrase

You're fine, Naomi. Everything is fine. I started telling myself this cop-out phrase. For a time, when I didn't have it in me to address it further, I'd pretend the phrase was true. *Everything* is *fine*, I'd snap back at my own thoughts.

About nine years into our marriage, I found myself in the middle of a spiritual crisis. My faith in God had been wavering in a way I'd never known before, and as a result, a lot of other things had begun to feel confusing and uncertain too. At the time I couldn't pinpoint one specific experience that had brought me to this breaking point. Looking back I realize I had let many small frustrations build up over time until they had nowhere to go but up and out.

At the foundation of one's faith, a culture often gets mixed in with the beliefs we hold to be true. This culture stems from loved ones in a family or church community. That group is likely full of well-intentioned people with the biggest and most open hearts imaginable. But we all fall short at times, and I'd begun to feel like my community of like-minded, faith-seeking individuals, as well as my faith-based leaders, were letting me down as I wrestled with questions both doctrinal and personal—in spite of having been an active, participating member of this same church body since I was a little girl, which was making my spiritual confusion all the more colossal. *Why have some things in my church changed when others haven't? Why do some in my church community act so mean or love to gossip so hatefully? Why does it feel like politics and religion are getting mixed?* These questions slowly chipped away at the church doctrines I'd held firmly, as well as the many faith-building moments I'd experienced with the people I loved within those circles of fellow believers. I began to feel ungrounded and disoriented as much change took place, while other topics remained untouched. I began to feel anxious and self-conscious attending my own worship meetings as I learned that many I sat beside each week were lashing out at, poking fun of, and fabricating stories about me. I began to feel shocked and blindsided with the political choices of people I respected in my religious community.

As the years passed, I tried to be patient while vulnerably seeking out answers. Two winters before, I'd met privately with a leader, desperate to be heard and understood and counseled on how to move forward. But my leader did not have any answers for me. And I felt brushed aside, as if he didn't care about my struggle with these issues. I didn't know what to do next, so I continued to hold it all in, often going through the motions outwardly as I told myself once again: *You're fine, Naomi. Everything is fine.*

Ultimately, my subconscious caught up to me. It was the Thursday before Christmas, and while my husband knew much about how I'd been feeling, I needed to get everything off my chest, and fast. I had to tell him everything.

As I whispered in bed beside him, a glow of lights sparkled

through our bedroom doorway from the living room Christmas tree. With our three little ones fast asleep in the adjoining bedroom, I quietly shared with Josh my questions and concerns, confessing how confusing everything around me had become.

I couldn't see his face well in the dark, but he held my hand, squeezing it gently at times when I'd break to cry. I usually don't like when our feet touch under the blankets, but that night I gripped mine around his, finding strength in his body heat as I tried to articulate what I needed to share with him.

He listened, rubbing my back as I talked and I cried. Crying isn't anything new for me. I cry a lot, but this crying felt different as the lump in my throat grew and then tightened. Panic I'd never known before consumed my entire being. I couldn't breathe. I was suffocating. I jumped from the bed, ripping off all my clothing, every single layer, as fast as I could until I was naked on the floor in the fetal position gasping for air. Josh jumped down onto the floor with me and held me.

My body shook. Even while being held, I seemed to lack any control to calm myself. I have no idea how long we embraced on the floor beside our bed, but at one point, I tried to open my eyes and couldn't, my eyelids heavy as my body slowly shut down. My head found its way to Josh's chest, where the beat of his heart steadied me.

In that moment, while feeling angry and betrayed by my faith, I was thankful for my husband. I could share my deepest truths with Josh, and he wouldn't debate me or tell me what I needed to do or not do. I clung to the belief that no matter what I said, he would still love me. He would still love me.

While our joint faith had always been the cornerstone of our family, something we'd both prioritized and held dear in our relationship, I found peace in knowing his love for me wouldn't shift even if I couldn't bring my faith back to where it once had been. The safe refuge he offered me was comforting in that moment, but even more so in the seasons ahead. I continued to navigate my spiritual journey, finding my beliefs on my own, and Josh's gentle, kind, and respectful actions backed his love each day without judgment, pressure, or expectations.

I gave myself a lot of space in the coming months, but I also began to acknowledge when I'd revert to my old mode of telling myself everything was fine. Instead of pushing my feelings away, I addressed each emotion fully as it arose. Sometimes I wasn't fine at all and I would let myself stay there, sorting through the many questions and doubts that surfaced.

I dug deep and asked myself what I really believed. Not because others in my life believed it, not because I'd been taught to believe it, not because I might be judged or shamed if I didn't believe it . . . but because it felt true to me. I had to go back to my core beliefs and start from scratch, completely breaking down what the culture had taught me and rebuilding my perceptions of the world around me (as well as the spiritual world I believe in and cannot see). I had to be patient with myself, which goes against my natural tendencies to ignore and move on. I had to decide what comes from God and what comes from mortals, what is assumed versus what is inspired. What is essential to salvation and what is a distraction in mortal life. And I had to remind myself that people (and even church leaders) are imperfect, just like me.

The following autumn I found my spiritual footing once again. I refocused on the happiness I feel knowing I am a spiritual daughter of Heavenly Parents who love me and have a plan for me. I am secure in knowing it's okay to still have questions and voice them (I have many many many) while trusting in something bigger than me. I've also accepted that I don't need to have all the answers at once, if at all. I root my life around the core belief that I am here to give of myself with faith in a greater purpose, while always finding beauty in His plan. Now, my faith is something I deeply believe and hold on to and cherish, a faith I feel more strongly and confident about than ever before, as I allot time to wrestle through the questions that had left me unsure.

While our outlook and beliefs and faith may differ, whatever it is you want to believe and value and build your trust in, I hope you are gentle with yourself as you seek it out. Don't let other voices try to mask your inner voice. Don't be afraid of what people will think if you stand up and ask the hard questions, but especially don't be afraid to ask yourself the hard questions too. No matter how you need to work through it, you'll sleep better at night knowing you aren't gaming yourself (even with babies who don't sleep—I promise).

And I hope you find that person—or perhaps people, if you are so fortunate in your life—who will cheer you on, support and believe in you, and give you the love you deserve, whatever path you choose to walk.

DATE: mostly autumn, 2017

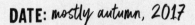 **LOCATION:** new york city

HAIRSTYLE: long. and somehow, despite throwing up my prenatal vitamin every single morning, the shiniest and healthiest it's been in ages

FAVORITE FOOD: the boston cream donut from dunkin isn't even that good, but it's on my mind daily (thanks pregnancy cravings)

NUMBER OF LITTLES: three. but this is where number four and number five come into play!

Baby A and Baby B!

We had just left my fertility doctor's office. It was a chilly October morning in the city, where the leaves were transitioning from green to yellow and orange hues, and I was wearing a scarf for the first time that season. We closed the clinic's front door and walked the three steps from the brownstone stoop to the sidewalk. I knotted my scarf around my neck as Josh turned his body toward mine. A siren loudly wailed past us. He took my hands and held them firmly in his. "Naomi, I'm so sorry . . ." he started.

I cut him off. I had to. I knew where he was going with his sentence. "Josh, it's okay! They're okay. There are still two babies and they're okay. I know it." I leaned in, my body shaking from the adrenaline and the hormones and maybe the cold. "I *know* it."

It had been our seven-week ultrasound appointment. The screen had shown two sacs in my uterus, but one was entirely empty—nothing but black in the sac where a baby should have been. The week prior, during my first ultrasound at the six-week mark, only one sac had appeared on the screen—two sacs didn't even register. And so, at this ultrasound, my doctor jotted "not viable" beside the empty sac in the exam-notes section of our ultrasound photo, with a big arrow pointing to the black oval where the embryo should have appeared. Then, as he'd done the week before, he gently prepped me for what he expected was a miscarriage of one or even both of the embryos, stating calmly each time that when one embryo slips this early on, it's likely to pull the other embryo with it. He again told me what to look for in the coming days—the bleeding, the pain. And I nodded my head from time to time as he spoke, but something inside me, deep down, knew there were still two.

Backing up a little bit for context, we were in the midst of our final round of IVF. We had been here before, even earlier that same year, with a failed IVF round, as well as years before that, in Washington, DC, when we first grew our family. (See "The Repetitive Birthday Wish" in part 4, if you haven't already.)

The road to this moment of standing on the sidewalk with my love, while bumpy and unsure and trying at times, had been paved with many tender mercies. For starters, while holding my newborn baby, Conrad, in the hospital a few years prior, minutes after his birth, I received a powerful and firm prompting from my Father in heaven that our family was not yet complete. As I looked down at my beautiful bundle of baby, this news didn't take away from my special first moments with Conrad in the slightest, but added to his magic. I felt God saw me and my heart, and I happily received His love and will for the unknown future.

Later, as Conrad's second birthday came and went and we weren't any closer to completing our family with a fourth little one, I became disappointed and confused. *What about that feeling I had at his birth and in the months that followed?* I also felt guilty for wanting another baby. *How could I, a mother of three healthy and thriving children, possibly long for and expect* another, when so many dream of a baby—just one baby—that doesn't come to be? What kind of woman did that make me? Am I justified in my feelings or just plain delusional? And who gets to decide the verdict? Shouldn't I shut up already since I have three? But how could I shut up the powerful feeling inside me that knew, with unwavering certainty, this family unit wasn't finished?

Through my experience I've learned that infertility, and secondary infertility, looks different, feels different, and is different for everyone. And rightfully so. Infertility is a sensitive subject, and it sucks, no matter how it differs from one person to the next.

Josh and I thought about, researched, and considered adoption during this time period. We prayed and meditated and explored all the possibilities for our fourth little one. In the end, we felt strongly about turning to a fertility doctor for help once again.

The morning after making the decision to try IVF once more, roughly a few weeks after Conrad's second birthday, my period showed up. It brought with it a side of hormonal cramping that felt twice as intense as usual, and while it made me moody, I also felt surprisingly hopeful.

Later that afternoon, I herded my three little ones from the playground into the back of a taxi, their scooters and helmets clunking about on the floor at our feet. Unsure where to start with executing our newfound plan, I decided to google my old fertility clinic in Washington, DC, as the taxi drove toward our apartment. Maybe my old doctor could refer me to someone in New York. I called. For the first time in my experience calling a doctor's office, someone picked up after two rings and didn't put me on hold. After explaining that I had been a patient several years back, the woman on the other end of the phone interrupted me. "Your doctor is no longer at our practice," she said.

"Oh. Okay . . . Um, well . . ." I staggered as I shuffled my hand around the handlebars of my children's scooters, the taxi making a sharp turn onto our block.

"He's in New York City now," she continued. "He opened his own practice there." It was just the tender mercy I needed to hear.

Fast-forward to about nine months later. I'd been in and out of countless appointments and procedures with my old, familiar doctor from DC, who now was an easy subway ride away in the city. We'd done a lot of medications. We'd done another egg retrieval, and we'd done another transfer with our best embryo. No luck. The embryo didn't stick. Though we had experienced this several years ago, Josh and I were heartbroken. The entire process takes an emotional, mental, and physical toll. And I was drained after losing our embryo. While standing in complete awe of modern medicine and the blessings it can bring, I wasn't sure how much sense it made to keep pushing. My heart knew our family was incomplete, but my body felt defeated and I was succumbing hard to that defeat.

With only two viable embryos remaining, we regrouped with my doctor and discussed trying one more time with one of the two embryos. If the transfer failed, we'd delay making another attempt with the final embryo until my body and mind recovered. My doctor would also run a new round of tests to see if something else was off that he hadn't detected previously.

We left his office and met with the nurse in a different room to review all the prepping for this next round. As they routinely did each round, she asked, "And how many embryos are you putting back in?"

"One," I replied without skipping a beat. "Just one," I confirmed again. She scribbled it on the chart she held. *One* was the game plan we'd decided on minutes before with my doctor for this new round, and *one* was also the number Josh and I had always imagined going into this.

As we made our way home, my mind remained in a steady state of prayer, as conversing with my Heavenly Father has proven to be a consistent and reliable practice in my life. Even when my faith hasn't been concrete and I question a lot of things, I can never discredit the power and direction and love I feel from my Heavenly Father when I pray. I believe in prayer. I believe in personal inspiration received through prayer. And so, a few days before our second embryo transfer and after saying my personal prayer before bed one evening, I knew as clear as day that there were supposed to be two. Two babies. Not just one. Two, arriving on this earth together. There were supposed to be two.

The thing is, my prayer had nothing to do with asking how many embryos to put back in. My prayer wasn't memorable or fancy. I'm sure I drifted at one point or other to a random thought that had nothing to do with my prayer because my attention span is bananas. What I do know is that after sharing with God what I so desperately desired, I acknowledged it was in His hands and I trusted whatever His plan might be for me and this embryo.

Two.

It was a lot to wrap my head around, but I couldn't shake the thought. It's hard to express how strong my prompting was to move forward with two.

Two felt like seven, or maybe even twelve. It felt impossible. Having twin sisters growing up, I'd gathered how hard it can be at times to *be* a twin, which scared me enough. I also doubted my ability to care for two babies at one time, along with my other three children. It didn't add up. But the direction was crystal clear and I couldn't deny that.

I waited until the following morning to tell Josh. He wasn't entirely on board when I shared the news, because he was experiencing similar worries and concerns. I asked him to think about it, to pray about it.

A day before the scheduled embryo transfer, Josh told me he supported my decision. He trusted me and my inspiration. And after a couple of calls to my doctor's office, they began prepping both of the final two embryos instead of one.

After implanting both embryos, the waiting game began until the six-week checkup, when we could first see the embryos on the ultrasound screen and know if the transfer had been successful. After what felt like twelve years, the week finally arrived. Week six—one sac on the ultrasound. Week seven—two sacs, one empty. At both appointments, no sign of a second embryo, no detection of a second heartbeat. No indication of a second baby whatsoever. All indications pointed to *one*. Not *two*.

While I was incredibly thankful to see the one embryo thriving and healthy on the ultrasound screen during those initial weeks, I was kneeling in prayer a lot after every ultrasound (and the long days in between), praying for both of my babies. I admit there were several moments in that time span when I was confused about why my initial prompting, so distinctively clear and direct, wasn't coming to fruition. But when I knelt in prayer, trying my hardest to talk with and understand this Being I had come to know as my Father in heaven, I felt close to God, and I felt close to my two babies.

At the eight-week ultrasound, both baby A and baby B appeared on the screen. "Well . . ." my doctor began, squinting his eyes and leaning in to the screen as he moved the probe on my belly a little to the right. "Well!" he repeated, looking bewildered as he studied the screen. "It looks like there really *are* two!" Two sacs, a baby in each one, both exactly on track with their eight-week measurements, with two of the strongest-sounding heartbeats accompanying them.

This time, after we walked the three steps from the brownstone stoop to the sidewalk, the crisp October air circling around us, Josh and I embraced in a tight hug, both letting the tears flow freely. *Two.* It felt so right, so real. Of course there are two. There were always supposed to be two. Together.

> *Tune out absolutely everything—and tune in to something Greater.*

Sometimes I feel like I don't have a grasp on anything (because at times I don't) and that I have much to learn with even the basics (because I do), but this experience taught me a humbling lesson to tune out absolutely everything—and tune in to something Greater.

I don't know what your belief system looks like, and I'm not here to tell you what your belief system *should* look like. But believing in *something* and prioritizing that *something* every single day can give life meaningful purpose and help steady you during life's tremulous moments. This unshakable experience in my life was the biggest reminder of that.

DATE: march 2019 ←———

LOCATION: the hallway of our church building

HAIRSTYLE: i keep saving pictures of perms to my pinterest board. i think it needs to happen.

FAVORITE FOOD: just made my way through all the snacks i brought to church for my kids, so hopefully no one is hungry in twenty minutes

NUMBER OF LITTLES: all five found their way into mama's room last night. i feel like we need a triple king bed.

Hallway Church
(It Mattered to Mama)

Sometimes I wonder what my kids will take away from having me as their mother. Will they remember only the times I lost my temper and my constant "Did you brush your teeth yet?" and "Unpack your lunch boxes and bring them into the kitchen already!" requests each day? Will it be the way I throw my pajama top on inside out most evenings, which I didn't notice until they started pointing it out to me? Or will it be how whenever it was Mama's turn to get them out the door for school drop-offs in the early morning, we'd have to sprint the entire three-minute walk, since punctuality isn't my strong suit? Was I gazing down at my phone too much? Preoccupied with tidying up and structured routines more than sitting down beside them on the floor and engaging?

I know the future holds plenty of conversations between the five children about Mama doing too much of this, too little of that. Even as I try to create a life for them where I diligently set aside my own childhood conditioning—pushing far away the many things I might have been conditioned to feel, think, and believe, and not allowing my own insecurities to trickle into my parenting style—they'll still have their own lists of frustrations and problems with how I did or didn't do many things. This is mothering. This is parenthood. This is life.

I fantasize that my kids' core memories of me will include things like my love of making up silly-worded songs and dancing with them in our living room each day, or how often we make homemade chocolate chip cookies together or never skimp on reading all the books before bed. That I was quick to listen, first to apologize, and always hugged them tightly.

A mama can dream. And when I do, I realize that one of my biggest desires for all five of my children is for them to remember that Mama believed in something. Mama believed in God.

I thought about this long and hard the other day while plopped on the carpeted flooring of the hallway in our church building. It was Sunday, and our church service was about a half hour into the sacrament portion of the meeting, beyond the closed doors of the chapel where I was not. Because instead, I wrangled two energetic, crawling ten-month-old sisters, Madalena and Beatrice, while trying to keep my cool as in the distance, four-year-old Conrad kept hitting the drinking fountain button, splashing water on his blue suit. Church for me more often than not the last eight years has consisted of "hallway church," which is basically attempting church worship on Sundays, but with a baby (or sometimes babies?!) and/or young children who have the attention span of exactly one pack of fruit snacks.

Attending our two-hour block of Sunday worship (which until recent worldwide changes in 2018 had always been a three-hour service!) has been a staple in my life since childhood and a cherished start to my week. Between singing many hymns with the congregation, participating in sacred ordinances like the blessing and passing of the sacrament emblems of bread and water to remember Christ, and being a part of inspiring and helpful discussions around an array of life topics and doctrine, weekly church services are something I highly value.

Our local church leadership (everyone from clergy members to Sunday school teachers) is based entirely on volunteers, so the deliberate dedication to one's congregation makes the community feel personal in many ways. And something I appreciate most about the setup is how my church community celebrates children and families with an exceptional Sunday school program for kids, as well as a "Nursery" program during the second hour for smaller ones once they are eighteen months of age. Even so, during those first eighteen months of my children's lives (and somehow many more months after, as many of my children haven't felt comfortable attending Nursery right away), most of my Sunday worship for the last eight years has involved tag-teaming little ones up and down the long halls alongside my husband, most often embracing, feeding, playing with, or hushing a little one somewhere on the floor outside the chapel and classroom doors.

On this particular Sunday I hadn't really attended the service because, per our usual routine, the girls and I had spent most of the two hours crawling around the confines of the church hallway, with our pile of board books and puffed baby snacks on the ground next to our stroller. I was feeling more bothered than refreshed or enlightened, as one might hope to feel upon completing Sunday worship, and wondered, *Why am I putting in all this effort to be here? Should I just take a rain check on attending church every week for eight more months until the girls are older and I can perhaps get something out of my church worship once more? Is this even worth it?*

I remembered a few years earlier bouncing a tired baby Conrad to sleep in the church hallway. I'd tried unsuccessfully to bring him into a Sunday school class that day, and between his loud squeals and tears, we had to excuse ourselves early. In the hallway, I'd felt annoyed, a scene that was already too familiar week after week with my third little one. On this Sunday two different congregation members paused briefly as they walked to different classrooms and sweetly shared the sentiment, "Just take him home! Go enjoy a nap or some alone time! You don't need to be here!"

Both gestures were sincere and kind, but deep down I knew I belonged at church. I knew that, despite not getting much out of the meeting, my family and I would still reap the blessings of putting God first on our Sundays. And more than anything else, I wanted to establish a habit for my children, from their earliest years, of observing the Sabbath day just like introducing vegetables into their diet, music into their days, and love into their lives. It's easy to get into the routine of making the effort only when you know you're going to get something in return, or worse, when it's convenient. And I knew myself well enough to acknowledge I could easily build a new habit that didn't include church at all on Sundays. I didn't want that, and I especially didn't want that for my children.

Early in our marriage, Josh and I made it a priority while traveling to seek out a church service. Sometimes that meant we didn't speak the language or know anyone attending. Even so, the meetings felt peaceful, uplifting, and special. As our family has grown and we've continued to travel, we have loved our shared moments attending church in a foreign country or community. The language or circumstance doesn't matter, because the spirit of love and unity surrounding our mutual faith feels strengthened.

So there I was a few years later, having made one too many laps around the building with my ten-month-old girls and getting absolutely nothing spiritual out of my Sunday. As I addressed the dilemma in my head about whether hallway church was worth it, I realized that it was. If I wanted, I could make it more meaningful and impactful with a positive attitude, by way of a carried prayer throughout my hallway pacing, reaching out to visitors sharing the hallway, or checking on and encouraging other parents with their arms full of tiny humans as they made their own rounds during "hallway church."

I'm in a season of life where church looks different with little ones, but even without being able to give proper attention to uplifting sermons or engage in any faith-building discussion, the experience can be valuable. Beyond the scope of my Sunday church dilemma, many seasons of life pull and tug at us, demanding our undivided attention, and it can feel challenging to know where to give our time and effort. Many chapters in life wrestle us in different directions, and even when any of the directions feel valid and good, we must learn how to embrace whatever the season throws our way, maintain a positive mindset, and make the best of things.

That day my biggest light-bulb moment came after I'd had this little epiphany as my older kids' primary classes let out. They made their way down the hallway to me, telling me all at the same time about a new song they'd learned, with accompanying sign language confidently performed right there on the spot. Their smiles radiated such joy and light that I felt fed despite not setting foot inside the chapel or a Sunday school classroom. But more than that, as Samson hugged my hips and looked up at me and asked if I'd had a good Sunday, I was able to answer him with a sincere yes, hugging him back. I knew my children understood how much it mattered to Mama—prioritizing church, my faith, my Heavenly Father.

I can't say with certainty that God or faith or church community will always be a focal point in my children's lives as they grow older and come into their own. But I hope I've given them the tools they need to understand the benefits and rewards of believing in something, of making and following

> I knew my children understood how much it mattered to Mama—prioritizing church, my faith, my Heavenly Father.

through with good habits and routines, of belonging and giving back to a community, of understanding the value of putting in the effort again and again—even when it could be easier to wait until it's more convenient. And when my children feel frustrated as seasons of life become busy and demand their attention, making it difficult to know what to prioritize and how, hopefully they'll remember a little bit of Mama doing what she could with her hallway-church season of life, because she believed in something—she believed in God.

PART NINE

TUNE OUT THE NOISE

DATE: february 2011

LOCATION: a hospital room in foggy bottom, washington, dc. every time we go back to dc to visit, my older two kids laugh at the idea that they were born in "foggy bottom."

HAIRSTYLE: i am a topknot girl—nice to meet you!

FAVORITE FOOD: it's hard to say, but i did shove a snickers

bar into my mouth postdelivery (two full days of laboring without eating had done me in) right before the nurse came back into the room to tell me that in about six hours they'd start me on an all-liquid diet, and i could probably eat solids in forty-eight hours. oops!

NUMBER OF LITTLES: my first baby girl is just a few hours old

The Sunny Side of Social Media

Our first official visitor at the hospital after Eleanor's birth was the same dear friend who threw me a baby shower a month earlier. We had a library-themed party, where each friend who attended graciously brought a copy of their favorite children's book. This helped us fill baby Davis's first-ever collection with treasured and best-loved classics, as well as new finds from trusted friends with impeccable yet varied taste. Considering my firstborn is never without a book in her hand nine and a half years later (we had to set rules about not reading while walking across busy intersections!), I'd say the baby-shower theme initiated something magical I'm forever thankful for.

I watched from my hospital bed as Josh proudly carried our baby girl across the room for my friend and her sweet husband to meet and hold. Seeing them huddled over her so tenderly made me emotional. In that moment I was thankful for so many things— for my new healthy baby, for being done with a challenging labor and birth, for medication and pebble ice, of course, but also for my good friend. I likely never would have met her if not for the internet and a comment left on my blog a few years prior, which in time sparked a beautiful off-line friendship that's still going strong today.

The comment that ignited our friendship was based solely on the baklava at the Hungarian Pastry Shop, the tiny and cool café at 111th and Amsterdam Avenue near Columbia University. (Naturally, you can see how this grew into a long-lasting friendship!) Her recommendation to try what is now one of my favorite treats fueled several further online exchanges, by way of blog comments and eventually emails, which about a year later led to an accidental first meeting in person at a car-wash fundraiser in DC.

I could smell the soapsuds hitting the wet pavement as I squinted in the morning sun to make out the face of the person talking to me. "Wait! I think I know you!" she exclaimed over the hood of my car. As we started chatting, I could hardly believe it. The weeks and months of our corresponding made our first (in real life) conversation feel as light and fun as the soap bubbles floating past us in the air. Meeting my internet friend at an early morning car wash was even more special than I could have hoped for.

The internet gets a bad rap sometimes. I understand why, as I've experienced its brutality, torment, and sorrow many times over. It's taken deliberate mental work to learn how to best acknowledge this sort of thing exists, and most likely always will, but also set it far aside from anywhere I ever want to be. The internet is such a weird place, but the online world can be phenomenal too.

She has a sunny side, the internet. A glorious, bright, and happy side that has brought unique connections into my life by way of online friends and community. I could sit here all day and list pages upon pages of the incredible people I've come to know in my years online, people who have touched my life in one way or another with their vulnerable and heartfelt words, videos, and photos. Online friends who have changed the way I approach many things, from seeing several topics in a different light to wanting to be a better wife, mother, friend, and human being. Some of these friends live halfway around the world, and we'll probably never meet in person, but I still appreciate how I've learned from them, been able to lean on them, and known them in a way. So when online friends have turned into friends off-line over the years, I hold the friendships especially dear.

Josh and I were strolling through SoHo one weekend afternoon when we were parents to only Eleanor and Samson. As we passed a park bench on a busy corner, we met a blog reader and her boyfriend, who approached us to say hello. She shared that she was originally from Ukraine, and with my Ukrainian heritage and obsession for Ukrainian food, I asked her, "Where do you go in the city for good pierogi?"

Within minutes she, her boyfriend, and our family of four were walking to her favorite Ukrainian restaurant a few blocks away. We shared great conversation over a delicious meal of some of my most favorite foods, and a few hours later, I couldn't stop smiling as our family caught the subway home. I'd been reminded once again of the warmth and friendship that live online when you seek them out in the right places and channels.

Sometimes when the world's frantic pace and noise feel a little too loud and fraught with tumult, I find myself pausing to reevaluate if sharing openly still makes sense or if the way I'm sharing feels right. When I pause, my mind recalls countless direct messages and comments on social media platforms, in personal emails, in blog comments, and in face-to-face conversations that have shown me how sharing parts of my heart has had a meaningful impact on other women around the world.

It would feel self-aggrandizing to elaborate on those stories and examples here, but just as the online world has helped me understand and navigate many things better, I have felt purpose in sharing about my life in helpful and sincere ways. Because when we realize our stories and experiences have the ability to help others improve a relationship or can encourage someone to be more intentional and kind in their marriage or mothering or to themselves, when we can help someone build a deep appreciation for their own life and family, and find ways to celebrate the everyday and love the life they live, it's all worth it. I believe that to my core, because I haven't just read the emails or messages; I've also been honored to meet, embrace, and talk face-to-face with many around the world I'm honored to call my online friends.

I can recount several service projects Josh and I have helped organize over the years, when we've invited our online community to come and volunteer with us and our family. Each time I'm in awe (but not surprised) at how quickly the spots fill up—usually within a matter of minutes, as our online community is anxious to take time out of their weekend itineraries and serve alongside us for several hours on a Saturday.

I recall the time we hosted a service project at the main warehouse in the Bronx for the Food Bank For New York City. It was during an unexpected snowstorm, and I anticipated the weather might result in a smaller turnout, but it didn't in the least. Despite the wintery conditions, we met readers who came all the way from Atlanta and Washington, DC, to help, as well as readers who were visiting on holiday from Spain and carved out time during their short stay to serve with us!

I'm thankful for the online friend I've never met in person but easily connected with over blogging, whose mothering I greatly admired while pregnant with Eleanor. I appreciated her willingness to tell it to me straight when I asked for her biggest tip as my first baby's due date approached. She replied to skip the overnight maxi pads and instead bring a pack of adult diapers with me to the hospital. At the time her direction sounded a little strange, because no one else in my circle had alluded to any sort of postpartum cleanup situation. But I trusted her guidance and made a special trip to the store to buy the adult diapers.

I often think back to how much I appreciated her candor, that she focused on something that perhaps wasn't as alluring a tip as "keep a journal" or "read this amazing book recommendation on sleep training." While not knowing me personally, she shared a piece of practical advice I've used four times over with the postpartum conditions that often follow a beautiful birth. All these years later, it's still the first thing I recommend to anyone who is about to have a baby.

I'm thankful for a blogger in California who, before I had children, influenced me to purchase my first pair of denim jeans in over five years (I hadn't been able to find a pair that worked for me). I'm thankful for the suggestions from so many when Josh and I have sought recommendations on restaurants and hotels and everything in between as we've traveled. For the shared holiday traditions, mothering tips, product picks, and heartfelt insights and perspectives on an array of topics, from politics to childrearing to fashion to creating to skin care and beyond.

The blog has brought incredible opportunities my way, like

an income or a fun collaboration or the chance to meet big people in high places. But at the end of the day, what I love most about blogging and social media is what I loved in its earliest days: the chance to connect with and be part of an enlightening community. Being a part of this community has saved me more than once. Several times when I've felt alone, someone has reached out and shared something she felt silly about sharing but had been prompted in her own way to send, without any idea how much I *did* need it and how timely it was.

When we use social media to meet amazing people and connect and lift and share, the internet is one of the brightest spots.

I appreciate the warmth the sunny side of social media has splashed in my life each and every day. I want to advocate for that sunny side and tell you right now that if you don't feel that warmth when you're engaging online, when you're reading or sharing or doing anything social media related, you might want to move away from the colder and shadier spots. Because I promise that when we use social media to meet amazing people—online, in person, or even unintentionally at a car-wash fundraiser—and connect and lift and share, the internet is one of the brightest spots. And as she seeps into our lives off-line, she keeps bringing that sunshine.

DATE: january 2018, roughly halfway through my twin pregnancy ←

LOCATION: coming at you live from my pillow!

HAIRSTYLE: hair painted ombre ends, and long bangs i'm almost parting down the middle

FAVORITE FOOD: popcorn made over the stove (the only way!), with extra butter and salt

NUMBER OF LITTLES: three, with two buns in the oven and a hot baby-name debate every night before bed

The Instagram Scroll

I slowly opened my eyes after hitting snooze for the fourth time. It was seven-something in the morning and I was half-asleep, the pillow still over my head as I grabbed my phone from the nightstand beside me. Practically habitual at that point, my thumbs and fingers opened Instagram without my brain so much as registering a fresh new morning's arrival. I began my day with a mindless scroll.

It wasn't my proudest era. I was halfway through my pregnancy carrying Beatrice and Madalena, with a fatigue and morning sickness so bold that leaving my bedside most mornings felt near impossible. But with my blaring, bright phone held inches away from my face before I'd even greeted my older three littles, something about the scene left me feeling icky morning after morning.

One morning I mentioned my frustration to Josh as I dramatically tried to sit up in bed, my phone glued to my hand after some twenty minutes of flipping through my 'gram while still lying horizontal. "I just don't know why I don't feel good," I complained. His response irked me before he even finished it, because at the root of his comment was something I already knew deep down.

"Do you maybe want to start charging your phone in a different room at night like you used to?" he said. "You know, so it's not a part of your morning routine."

Maybe the nausea-and-dry-heaving-and-growing-two-tiny-humans situation played a small role in the way I felt each morning, but truth be told, morning sickness was a freaking cover for the numbing effect my phone was having on me. Robbing minutes away from beginning each day with an intentional prayer, or a moment of stretching my persevering body, or perhaps meditating and writing in a gratitude journal and setting deliberate goals, even the simplest, for my day. I mean, I don't think anyone should be an overachiever during pregnancy, but I also don't think it's an excuse to let something else take hold of the very best of you, and in doing so, potentially harm you in the process.

As Josh had alluded to when offering his suggestion, I'd been here before, not too long ago. I already knew what action and steps on my part were needed to declutter my morning phone routine, as well as my evening phone routine. What I'd done then was simple enough to do now: charge my phone in a different room at night and not bring it into my bedroom to sit beside (and distract?!) me on my nightstand.

Like most hard-to-break habits, it wasn't the easiest feat to conquer at first, but eventually my plan showed great progress. I didn't crave the phone in the late evenings before sleep, and the early hours of the day felt lighter, almost more freeing, when my phone wasn't part of my morning practice. Over time the separation helped pace my daily phone intake, too, since my every movement during the long day often took place with my phone resting in the back pocket of my jeans, if not clenched in my left fist. I didn't check my phone as much, so I didn't feel like I needed to scroll it 24/7.

Yet somehow I picked the habit back up as I spent most of my hours sick and pregnant in bed. Scrolling again for scrolling's sake. Here I was again.

But let's discuss that "infinite scroll," whether on Instagram or TikTok or Facebook or some other platform. I don't think it has to be categorized as entirely bad. I'm a big advocate for the good that social media spreads when it's a tool used the right way. An Instagram scroll can be full of inspiration and aspiration. It can connect us to one another as we navigate life's hurdles, with a glimpse at images and topics explored by others in our chosen online community, traversing the same situations around the world. When we think of our goals for using social media, hopefully we want to connect with family and friends; people who align with what we seek, give, and cultivate; and others who challenge us to grow.

Like all things in life, moderation is important. And at times—as the generation for which social media came to life while we were navigating pivotal moments—we can forget that it isn't everything.

Back in 2005, when Facebook wasn't anything like it is today (and some might argue when it was in its prime), I walked around my dorm with a fellow classmate, asking students to sign a petition. We were trying to have the Juilliard School recognized through acquiring a certain number of signatures, so we could join the ranks of the original Facebook—the one to which, at the time, only a handful of elite universities were given access. We wanted to be a part of it, despite being a small liberal arts conservatory not known for our sororities or sprawling campus grounds. The world back then felt exciting, with dial-up internet, AOL chats, and now this new, inviting world of Facebook we soon received approval to create profiles for. We were pre-smartphones, pre-phones-taking-photos, pre-using-your-phone-for-anything-beyond-calling-and-simple-text-messages.

From there, social media use snowballed a bit for me. While I was blogging in my early twenties, YouTube grew in prominence, then Twitter, then Pinterest, then Instagram and others. There was no handbook for how to navigate life with these new social media tools, but as our phones began to advance, with built-in cameras and easy access to the internet from anywhere, the landscape of our new normal shifted quickly.

I saw both the benefits and the drawbacks, and I felt I had a good grasp and well-intentioned boundaries in place, not only for what I chose to share publicly but also for what I chose to consume. Sometimes it would get tricky, as I'd find myself thirty videos deep down a rabbit hole on YouTube or so far back on an Instagram scroll, I didn't even know what I'd originally clicked on that got me there, but the balance felt relatively stable.

Until at times it didn't. Like when the Instagram scroll became all-consuming and I'd mindlessly open the app and scroll because it's what I'd trained myself to do—consume just to consume, with no end goal or motive or purpose. I enjoyed keeping up with friends' and families' adventures through their tiny squares, but once I'd caught up on everything in my feed, I'd scroll the "Explore" page of the Instagram app because I wanted more tiny squares to keep tabs on. The habit built a new nervousness within me when I didn't have my phone within arm's reach.

After my conversation with Josh about charging my phone in a different room, I knew I needed to take further steps to safeguard my mental space and be in control of my phone habits. I needed to get back to and understand the root of why I scrolled at all, as my content intake needed to be checked. So I opened up my favorite app and looked things over. The next thing I did was a bit drastic: I started unfollowing hundreds and hundreds of the social media accounts I followed at the time, from home interior and fashion brands to travel sites and celebrities to acquaintances and people I didn't interact with anymore. Because I realized that while I still enjoyed many of the accounts I was ingesting each day, I was sucked into the mentality that I needed to make sure I saw *all* of the posts, the updates, the stories and videos, and even the comments on particular channels, and this activity thus required a ridiculous amount of my time.

I believe in building community and supporting others on these sites, but I knew I needed to set boundaries. Although I was nervous I might offend others by unfollowing accounts I'd subscribed to for years, sometimes letting go for your own time, mental health, and purpose is more important. I didn't need to keep up with more than six hundred Instagram accounts every day, and in making my Instagram scroll significantly smaller (even when some accounts were inspiring and lovely and helpful—we could spend all day soaking in the amount of good people and brands and businesses on social media!), my time on my phone was sliced substantially. The revamped scroll felt like a positive experience, the right amount of intake before looking back up at my life and living it once again, away from my screen.

Just as we determine how we spend our time in real life, curating our online experiences to get the most out of them will help us build stronger connections both online and off-line. Maybe you don't need to unfollow all of the accounts to improve your social media intake, but remembering that what you consume becomes a big part of *you*, fill your feed appropriately. Make your Instagram scroll a worthwhile and meaningful experience with a daily or weekly time limit that you set for yourself.

> *Curating our online experiences to get the most out of them will help us build stronger connections both online and off-line.*

You don't need to follow any accounts that don't uplift or teach or stretch you to grow. If it ever makes you feel less than, unqualified, empty, unhappy, or even just meh, you don't need to consume it anymore. You don't need to apologize or justify why you won't anymore either. Your social media is *your* social media for a reason. And when you follow the right accounts for *you*, social media can be a place where you are well fed, loved, inspired, challenged, and encouraged.

DATE: the last dozen years as "taza"

LOCATION: sitting alone in my car in washington, dc, to now, typing alone on my bed in arizona (odds are against me being alone much longer—i think my family just realized i snuck away to my bedroom)

HAIRSTYLE: a simple pony and i am desperate to find a couple of bobby pins for my bangs. i swear those things grow legs in the night and walk away.

FAVORITE FOOD: i was thinking we should be tacos for halloween, if that gives you any context for what i can't get enough of lately . . .

NUMBER OF LITTLES: five, but some are starting to be not so little!

A Thin Skin

I've heard variations on a certain phrase countless times over the past decade. The intentions behind it are always sincere, with the words meant as a compliment, a badge of honor if you will. "You must have such a thick skin," people will say, sometimes acknowledging that they aren't sure how I do it or that they could never do it. Because at the end of the day, someone who shares openly on the internet about anything personal, sharing that can be met with critics and trolls and an array of negative commentary each day, can only mean one thing: you must have the thickest of thick skins.

Actually, I have a very thin skin. And I've finally stopped trying to change that.

I had a hard time in the beginning. While much of the online world can be a bright and happy place, a big part of me had trouble letting go of the one negative comment out of every one hundred positives received and not fixating on each and every harsh word. I'd try to act tough, pretend I didn't care, pull out that head-to-toe skin made of thick armor I'd hear others talk and write and blog about. But most of the time, I felt like Peter Pan trying to sew on his shadow with a bar of soap. It was impossible.

A couple of years into sharing, I received my first comment that wasn't constructive criticism but instead was thirteen sentences of full-blown, spewing, personalized hate. It took me a few hours to even see the comment, which by then had a full discussion underneath it, with people either agreeing with said comment or defending me. As fast as my fingers could find the button, I deleted the initial comment and the thread of discussion below it, reciting the thirteen sentences to myself as I did so and feeling wrecked all over again long after it disappeared from my blog. The email came in shortly after. It was lengthy, but the part that still stands out from the message is the phrase "If you can't stand the heat, get the hell out of the fire!"

This is by no means harsh compared to other things I've been emailed or messaged. This is rather kindly put, considering what's come my way since—notes with vivid violence, encouragement to kill myself, slanderous suggestions, and explicit exhortations I won't reproduce here. But this phrase got me thinking: When you share your heart publicly on the internet, why is it assumed you have no feelings, no boundaries, no right to privacy? That you're suddenly fair game for the nitpicking and dissecting of those who choose to remain entirely anonymous behind their screens? I know I'm supposed to be chill about it as a very minor "public figure" and accept that, in my position, whatever I say and do will be ripped apart, but come on now. Are we really going to set the bar that low for how we comment, discuss, and interact with others online?

There's a stark difference between constructive criticism or a plaintive opposing opinion and the polluting of one's comment section with negative, unhelpful, untrue, or downright mean comments. Over the years, it has been an education to have readers share differing opinions and feedback, to help me gain new perspective and understanding on an array of topics. I have appreciated the open dialogue and informative approach when the discussion is redirected in a explanatory way so I (and hopefully others) can grow and learn and change my behavior with new insight. It's one of the things I feel most fortunate to have gained with my experience in the online space.

But then there's the mean-spirited, unhelpful, and downright vicious commentary. I don't know how anyone can engage with it and feel justified in doing so. The first time I accidentally happened upon a discussion thread where I was the sole topic, skimming hundreds upon hundreds of snarky and bullying comments focused entirely on me and my blog, I wasn't sure I'd ever recover. I didn't know dark and brutal places like that existed on the internet, and it crushed me as I sat alone in my parked car on Capitol Hill in Washington, DC, reading on as anonymous commentators analyzed everything from the size of my chest to the size of my teeth, poked fun at my writing, called my husband inappropriate names, boldly shared false facts about my life, my family, my thoughts, and even going so far as to share my current and past addresses so people could come by and watch me to see how supposedly fake I was—or do much worse.

A few months later a fellow blogger told me she checked forums and sites like these daily, where she also had her own threads, so she'd know how to "curve" her content and make the snarky commenters like her more. I knew the hate sites and forums were wrong, but her approach felt more wrong. A bunch of trolls who spent their free time putting others down on the internet wasn't the kind of crowd I wanted to win over, and trying to cater anything to them or altering one's behavior, appearance, or speech solely for others' approval doesn't seem like the most solid foundation for a happy life. Snarky internet-land aside, I also was trying my hardest not to give too much weight to the positive, over-the-top complimentary comments I sometimes received. Because while they'd make me feel nice and good and all for a minute, I knew their potential to be as destructive as the hurtful and hateful comments if I gave too much emphasis to others' validation of me and my choices.

The internet can be an awesome place and a productive tool for building connections and community across geographies, but it's not a structure from which you should derive your self-esteem. Not everyone is going to love you. Not everyone will hate you either, and at the end of the day it's absolutely okay, because the feedback isn't about you anyway. It's usually about other things— it's usually about the other person.

We can't let the feedback consume us or direct our next actions, words, or steps. It's hard—especially when you want to be liked, as I have over the years—to not let others' loud commentary creep into how we define ourselves. However, when I look back at the times I've been happiest in my life, they're when I've loved myself for me without anyone else telling me what I should or shouldn't think of myself.

Someone can comment online ad nauseum that I'm a terrible mother or I love one child more than the rest, that I should get a "real job" or focus on this issue more than that one, that my jaw is too manly or my feet are too big, or this or that or whatever it is they're fixated on that day. But I know I'm a good mother and love all of my children to the moon and back, that my jaw works fine and my feet are strong, that I work hard and try to serve and help others and make an impact. When you know and love yourself in that way, you can see the commentary for what it is: a whole lotta noise. All the other stuff—the fluff and hate and static noise of the world around us—should be like water beads trickling down the outside of an umbrella. While the noise might not quiet entirely, you don't hear it as much, because the volume dial is back in your hands and not in anyone else's.

When I see a hateful comment, something that has helped me tremendously is reminding myself that there's a person on the other side of the device, a person with feelings and insecurities and frustrations, like me. Someone who cries and (hopefully) laughs and is doing their best too. They are human.

> *While the noise might not quiet entirely, you don't hear it as much, because the volume dial is back in your hands and not in anyone else's.*

And with respect to ourselves, I heard a great quote that has been attributed to Glennon Doyle: "Just a reminder that there's not two of you—internet you and real you. There is just one real you. Which means if you're not kind on the internet, you're not kind." I think it's a great prompt for all of us to check ourselves often online, as we might off-line.

My biggest takeaway from the hate and exaggerated emotions I've experienced on the internet is to refocus my intentions, both online and beyond. Am I using this platform to uplift, to be a bright spot in someone's day, to be kind, to be helpful? When I log off, do I feel good about what I've said and shared online? Was it worth my while? And was it worth theirs—those who take the time to visit my blog or social channels? I certainly hope so.

At the end of the day, online and off, some people will like you and some people won't. I *do* wish all of them well—the authors of generous and thoughtful comments as well as those who conceive unkind and hateful replies, though I hope the latter are able to eventually let go of the angst. And although I've tried to grow the thickest of skins over the years, I've realized I actually like me best the way I've always been, which is with a pretty *thin* skin and a lot of feelings that I don't like bottled up, unable to feel. I hope to keep leading a life full of kindness, empathy, and love, and continue focusing on who *I* am and why *I* share.

It's possible to thrive in an online world with a thin skin, even in an online world that's sometimes hostile and wants nothing more than to get under that skin. You just have to know who *you* are and why *you* share. It's not always easy, but I strive for this mentality and I've greatly benefited from it when I've fully embodied it. And when you're able to do that—to see the praise and harsh criticism that come your way for what they are and not let them define any part of you—I have amazing news for you: it doesn't even touch your skin.

PART TEN

PACK YOUR (DIAPER) BAGS

DATE: early summer of 2017

LOCATION: new york city, after two weeks in the rocky mountains out west ⟵

HAIRSTYLE: growing out the bangs but also finding the scissors at midnight every few weeks, so . . .

FAVORITE FOOD: will find any excuse to get myself a helping of rice pudding from rice to riches in nolita. doesn't matter the hour. hello, postmates!

NUMBER OF LITTLES: my three musketeers! but often being confused for a small army of over a dozen musketeers by the noise level alone

New York City, Our Backyard

We'd just returned from vacation. With new freckles dotting our noses and bold tan lines to prove it, our family had spent two weeks taking in the fresh mountain air, green forests, and clear rivers of America's Wild West. On the taxi ride home from the airport, with my little ones tucked beside me, I held my breath at that first view of the New York City skyline, where the glittering lights beckoned against the darkened sky.

As the taxi navigated the busy streets, I tried to center myself, reexamining how I felt to be *home*. It's something I've done frequently over the years, having small moments to check in with myself and evaluate my feelings to make sure *it* still feels right, whatever it is we're doing.

Looking out the cab window, we were welcomed back to the city by mounds of trash bags lining the streets for pick up. Despite the late hour, the driver fought traffic because of construction delays, and we covered our youngest's ears when a stream of sirens screeched past. Even so, my butterflies fluttered in full force as we turned each corner, approaching our neighborhood. It felt unbelievably good to be back, to be back home, and I was thankful for the comforting reassurance. But I held back from sharing my thoughts and instead kept a close eye on my children, trying to discern if they felt the same or perhaps the opposite—disappointment at being back in the city, back to small spaces, loud sirens, and an awful lot of stairs.

"So now that you have kids, when are you leaving the city?"

I was asked this question when we had only two kids. I was asked this question more frequently once we added our third child. And now that we've hit five—Eleanor, Samson, Conrad, Madalena, and Beatrice—the question is inevitable. But it still fascinates me. Somehow there's this stigma that city life and child-rearing cannot go hand in hand. The question usually doesn't faze me, but in that moment, as we returned from such a merry experience out west, the stigma threatened to engulf me. Was it time for us to leave the city? Did the kids need a private backyard, as so many people had suggested through the years?

My mind wandered back to a few days before, when my little ones' joyful bodies galloped freely along the mountainside, their laughs filling the grassy meadow as they playfully tackled one another to the soft ground. The doors to the home we had rented remained wide open throughout the days. "There's no dead bolt!" my confused five-year-old Samson animatedly announced when closing the door one evening. You'd think he'd just seen Santa Claus ride by, his face full of amazement at such a thing as a front door with no dead-bolt lock to secure it. Also, we should probably discuss the stars in the sky. I love my twinkling city skyline to the moon and back, but there is something dreamy about standing with your children and looking up into a pitch-black skyline filled with bright and beaming stars. Especially when their version of the song "Twinkle, twinkle, little star, how I wonder what you are . . ." goes something like "Twinkle, twinkle, traffic light, shining on the corner bright. Red means stop, green means go, yellow means very slowwww . . . ," as Conrad came home from the first day of kindergarten singing loudly (and proudly—thank you for that, Conrad).

As we neared our street I anxiously listened as my children called out familiar landmarks.

"There's the school!"

"I see the museum!"

"Look! The crepe place! It still has its lights on!"

"I spy with my little eye . . . Ray's Pizza!"

Each sighting proved more exciting than the one before. Samson chimed in with a celebratory horn sound, and we all laughed. But it wasn't until we'd lugged all the bags up the stairs and turned on the lights of our apartment that their eyes filled with delight.

Conrad ran straight to his bed and hugged it profusely. "Bed, I love you! I've missed you! I'm so happy to see you!" My other children skipped around, getting reacquainted with their toys, their stuffed animals, all their favorite things.

"It feels so good to be back," Eleanor shared as she plopped onto the sofa with a book she'd grabbed from the bookshelf. "I love being home."

A sense of gratitude rushed down my spine. While I knew I still loved calling the city home, I hadn't realized until that moment how much I deeply needed to hear proof of my children's love for home too. Proof that not just wide-open spaces with big backyards can feel enchanting and special but small apartments with shared bedrooms and no backyard can feel that way too.

In addition to commenting about the need for a yard, it's

not unusual for people to suggest our kids need their own bedrooms. At times I've worried that our children are being cheated in some way by having to share such a tight space. But people all around the world share bedrooms and small spaces without a second thought. While personal space is important and we try to give that to each of our kids in healthy doses, the close quarters have strengthened our family bond. And while I've done my best to make their space a fun, clean, colorful place, with twinkling lights strung across the ceiling and their favorite books organized beside their beds, the material things don't dictate the value of their upbringing. How we as a family interact in this space (and outside of it) matters most.

It's about the tone we use with one another when communicating. It's about playing beside our children on the floor, really connecting with them. It's about reading to them, hugging them, and then hugging them more. It's about creating a safe space where we all feel free to sing and laugh, but where we can also feel comfortable crying and saying, "I love you." A place where we can be completely ourselves, ask questions and not be judged, talk through problems or frustrations, forgive and find forgiveness. Anyone can create this sense of home, whether in a small city apartment where our children share a bedroom or in a large home outside the city with plenty of room to spare. Because it isn't about the space—it's about what's taking place inside of it.

> It isn't about the space—it's about what's taking place inside of it.

While I imagine a big, private backyard would be very fun for our brood of five children (or any child), the city does offer public parks with plenty of room for them to explore, run, play, and be kids. There's no mowing a lawn or pulling weeds at home, though our family has enjoyed volunteering in a community garden. In the winter months, we don't have to plow the snow in the driveway but still get to enjoy the city's sledding hills! And we have loved making new friends nearly every time we visit one of the city playgrounds.

Shifting our mentality away from lacking a private backyard for our children allowed us to focus on what the city experience can offer them instead, from vibrant arts, culture, and delicious food (not to mention delivery even at 2:00 a.m.) to the diverse people and an energy that can't be replicated elsewhere. When I start to doubt my choices as a mother, I zoom out and remind myself there isn't one way to raise a child, one formula for how it should be done. And there certainly isn't one place or environment that fits all children, parents, or caregivers.

Regardless of where we all land, we can choose to pull from every resource our environment offers. Then we can supplement those resources with an abundance of love, living every day to honor and care for those precious souls we hold in our arms.

DATE: november 2012

LOCATION: our last day in venice, italy

HAIRSTYLE: long and straight, parted down the middle with grown-out bangs!

FAVORITE FOOD: i enjoy stuffing my turkey and cheese sandwich with doritos

chips and ranch dressing and now you'll probably never take me seriously the next time i dish out a food recommendation, right?!

NUMBER OF LITTLES: my one-year-old eleanor with those adorable pigtails and baby samson with that wee mohawk

We're Going on an Adventure!

A loud knock on our hotel-room door woke me and all three of my travel companions. I attempted to soothe my toddler, Eleanor, and six-month-old Samson back to sleep as Josh answered the door. He and the concierge exchanged several energetic sentences in Italian before Josh returned holding up makeshift plastic boots, compliments of the hotel.

We first saw the flooding as we made our way down the hotel's winding staircase. An employee stood in the lobby with what looked like an ill-equipped vacuum cleaner, nonchalantly attempting to remove said water, about a foot and a half deep, pooling in every direction. The visual is permanently etched into my head all these years later, as I still wonder about the safety of such a venture.

It was our family's final day in Venice, Italy—and the first day in several years when the city experienced a historic rise in their waters, flooding not only the streets and canals but also shops, restaurants, and hotel lobbies, which were under nearly five feet (150 centimeters) of *acqua alta* (Italian for "high water"), thanks to unusually well-aligned high tides and a surprising amount of rainfall. When we went to sleep the night before, we'd set our alarms with just enough time to get to the airport for our flight back to the United States. But that didn't include any time for swimming!

"I wonder if your black leggings can fit me," Josh said once we were back in our hotel room, as we problem-solved how to make the ten-minute trek to the water-taxi dock off Piazza San Marco, since the streets and train tracks to the airport were flooded. I started searching around in my backpack for the leggings.

"I really can't believe you talked me into this," I said. I didn't mean the trip to Italy—you don't have to twist my arm for the chance to eat homemade pasta and see Michelangelo's *David* in person. I was referring to clocking in a little under two weeks in a foreign country, with two extra-small children and one large backpack each (so two packs total for all *four* of us) and a double stroller as our only luggage. Packing this light meant Josh only brought one pair of pants, and as we were about to embark on an impromptu water adventure on our way to the airport, we both realized that sitting on a plane in drenched denim for ten hours didn't sound like much fun.

"I know. Isn't this exciting? What an adventure, traveling with no pants!" Josh said before he jumped and wiggled and danced his way into my leggings. We both had tears streaming down our faces from laughter at the sight of it.

"You look great, Josh," I joked as we strapped on our new plastic-garbage-bag boots that extended up to our kneecaps. "The boots really complete your travel outfit!"

Josh wore his backpack on the front of his body, strapped Eleanor in the baby carrier on his back, and pushed the empty stroller toward the taxi dock. I followed him with my backpack on my back and Samson cradled in my arms. I smiled at sweet Eleanor, who kept looking back at me as she happily pointed at the water and clapped her hands enthusiastically. During some stretches of our march, I'd do my best to mask my inner gasps at the sight of our stroller seats fully immersed in water. If you've known me for even a short time, you know how I can't seem to shut up about my double stroller and all it can do. I think this trip was what solidified my love of my side-by-side push-chair, which—I'd like to point out—made a solid recovery, with no damage beyond squeaking loudly for a few weeks after our Venice water-walk. Anyway!

Once at the airport, Josh and I took turns holding the children while each of us changed in a bathroom. We peeled off our soaked leggings and attempted to wipe the dirty canal water off our legs and feet before putting on our only pairs of dry pants. We hugged and high-fived before boarding our flight home. "I love adventures with you," I said, as Eleanor ate crackers on my lap and Josh helped Samson with his pacifier.

We alternated sharing highlights from our trip, which included me trying to discreetly pump breastmilk outside St. Peter's Basilica in Rome and locking up our double stroller on the street. I had to lock it up beside a motorcycle in Cinque Terre after we failed to carry it up six flights of stairs to our small guesthouse rental, which overlooked the multicolored palazzos stacked on the cliff around the tiny bay of Riomaggiore on the Mediterranean Sea. One of our favorite memories had been watching twenty-one-month-old Eleanor chase pigeons outside the Colosseum and finish off every gelato ice cream cone we handed her, determined to never spill a drop.

We could laugh now at the two-and-a-half-hour train ride

from Florence to La Spezia, where we hadn't realized we booked tickets without seats and were in a standing-room-only car. And somehow, despite having to cancel a highly anticipated dinner reservation in Rome because two little ones were done adventuring on that particular day, we agreed that our most treasured meal and memory of the trip coincided with room service later that evening. Eleanor entertained us by wearing a silver room-service lid as a hat, holding two spoons, and babbling away at her little brother, Samson, who gazed up at her with the biggest eyes full of awe while we looked out the hotel window at the Colosseum and Rome rooftops.

Despite that specific night going nothing like we'd imagined, it topped the trip for us both. The sunset over Rome from our window, our children covered in pasta sauce, and Josh and me leaning our tired heads back on the bedframe, sharing a smile, and learning a valuable lesson about the need to "go with the flow" during our first international trip with young children.

"Was it worth it?" a friend asked when we returned home, trying unsuccessfully to mask her conviction that we'd wasted time and money going to Europe with young children. "I mean, with the kids. Do you think you'd ever do it again?"

I didn't even have to think about it. "Totally," I replied.

It is absolutely, totally, completely worth it, traveling anywhere with young children. As we've added three more kids to our family and more trips around the world, both near and far, the travel experience has helped us create a special bond as we explore, learn, and try new things in new destinations together. I've heard the argument that travel is best once the kids are much older and can remember the experiences for themselves, and I understand that approach in many regards. But if there's an opportunity to expose little ones to different smells, tastes, languages, people, cultures, and traditions in their early years, I believe this will help shape them as human beings, leaving a lasting impression as they grow to someday contribute to our world in meaningful ways.

Most of all, Josh and I hope these experiences will help our kids recognize that our way of doing things isn't the only way, an important awareness to have while navigating school, work, government, church, and family. Also, developing a built-in sense of flexibility from an early age, going with the flow and making anything into an adventure, can have a special impact on how they approach their lives now and once they're on their own.

Travel aside, a mentality of getting out and seeking adventure with our family has been a big priority since our kids were infants. Heading out of our neighborhood to hike together, picking apples or blueberries or whatever fruit is in season, packing up the car for a full day of exploration, seeing where the drive takes us—we've enjoyed many low-key and inexpensive ventures together too.

Of course, any outing with small kids—whether a trip to a faraway land or a day trip out of your neighborhood—must be approached differently than if you're traveling only with adults. It's unlikely you'll cover as much ground, and the itinerary needs to include explorations that appeal to the tiny members of your adventuring crew. I admit the outings felt like more of a breeze when our children were babies and didn't care much about how many hours we wandered through a museum or what was on the menu at a restaurant or drive-through.

Even so, as we've sought out specific activities geared toward our elementary school–aged kiddos, we all usually have a wonderful time. We've graduated from Gladiator School in Rome, where Eleanor, Samson, Conrad, and even Josh completed a rigorous history and physical-training course before participating in a scary battle in full gladiator armor while Beatrice, Madalena, and I cheered them on from makeshift colosseum-style seating. We brought knight and dragon costumes with us to a castle in Switzerland, so the kids could enjoy a day full of make-believe as we wandered the grounds. We've made homemade churros in Mexico and handmade pasta in Florence, by seeking out cooking classes geared toward children. We've attended a puppet show at the Sydney Opera House in Australia and cleared an entire day's itinerary of sightseeing at the end of the two hours we'd allotted at the London Transport Museum, once we realized our kids would be in heaven staying put to explore all things transportation for the remainder of the day. We had to drag them away at closing time.

These types of activities aren't necessarily first on my list when making up our travel schedule, but somehow, after all is said and done and we return home, they tend to top our list of things we loved most.

No trip with kids has ever gone smoothly. We've had meltdowns outside the Louvre in Paris, what felt like a million mosquito bites on our ankles (I didn't think about the ankles when applying bug spray!) after a day at Machu Picchu in Peru. We've lost shoes in Amsterdam and had kids declare they "love pasta" and also "hate pasta" during the course of the same meal in Italy. And a trip never seems complete without one throw-up extravaganza. Then again, this is life with kids no matter where we are: home, the grocery store, an airport, or the beginning/middle/end of a trip.

I acknowledge the privilege our family has, with the resources and time to travel together. From the beginning, a lot of how we've structured our travel has been prioritizing experiences and adventures over physical gifts. We stretch our dollars as far as we can when exploring a new destination by subscribing to cheap airfare and deal sites, traveling during off-peak seasons, and researching ahead of time to get the most out of tourist sites, passes, and tickets.

That said, I'm a firm believer that you don't need to get a passport stamped to have an adventure with your family. The true luxury lies in grasping whatever scenario is around you and turning it into what you want it to be. An afternoon of running errands to the post office and grocery store with little ones doesn't have to only be an afternoon of running errands. For me, many an errand has been an adventure in its own right, searching for alphabet letters along the store aisles or putting on pretend spy glasses as you seek a sneaky mission.

You don't need to get a passport stamped to have an adventure with your family.

Our kids have sported full astronaut attire and superhero costumes while out grocery shopping, and Conrad has come very close to having his long dragon tail caught between the subway train doors when he accompanied me to vote downtown one year. As I've played along and allowed the adventure to follow us into ordinary afternoons around the neighborhood, I've witnessed the best giggles and stories born as fun memories have been made.

As parents, we have the ability to foster the creativity our little ones arrive here with and help them keep that sense of awe and excitement and magic alive! As I've slowed down and embraced the puddle, paused to wave at the construction trucks, and eliminated phrases like "Hurry up!" from the words I say to my children, I've learned how the adventure can be just as special in our own living room and backyard (or city yard!) as where the plane lands.

———

I often think back to our first family trip to Italy, when the canals in Venice flooded. My biggest takeaway from the adventure, with a toddler and baby and two carry-on backpacks, was that keeping my expectations flexible and making the most of the circumstances are key to having an incredible time together, one we can reflect on fondly for years to come. I've carried this approach into other family adventures, understanding how traveling (or adventuring) together shapes our perspectives and our children's mindsets in positive ways, and how cultivating a world of wonder wherever we are can be rewarding in its own fantastic way too. While sometimes I still get flustered wanting things to go just right, and right on time, with idyllic weather and no spills and especially no tears, I can see the benefits of putting on the wrong-sized leggings and wading through the canal water.

DATE: june 2019

LOCATION: high in the sky between LA and NYC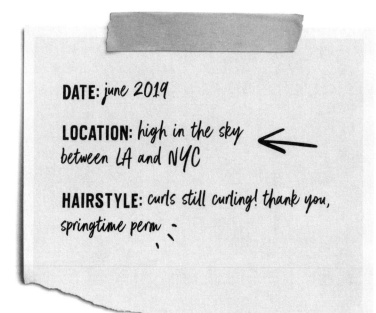

HAIRSTYLE: curls still curling! thank you, springtime perm :

FAVORITE FOOD: i plowed through an entire bag of skittles in a span of five minutes on this flight, so probably anything but skittles

NUMBER OF LITTLES: traveling with the smallest two out of five this trip

One Mama, Two Babies, and Six Hours in the Air

I jokingly texted my girlfriend, "Tell me honestly: Is the airport a terrible place to have my first-ever glass of wine?" For someone who doesn't drink, the thought did cross my mind ever so briefly as I walked up and down a long stretch of LAX with my twelve-month-old twin daughters—Madalena strapped to my chest in a baby carrier and Beatrice plopped on my hip. After our original flight back home to New York had been canceled several hours earlier, this second transcontinental flight we'd been booked on had been delayed for a second time in two hours. The three of us had already devoured the snack stash for the entire flight home and depleted all of the baby-wipe supply. And we were down one adorable outfit because of a blowout that went straight up the back instead of into the diaper. But we were also doing our best to make the most of our fourteenth lap around terminal 7, while waiting to board our flight.

About a week earlier, I'd flown to LA with my two barely toddlers to meet up with a few girlfriends from college and their little ones. (We'd all given birth within a year of one another.) It would have been fun to reunite in the city where we all created many important memories and forged our bond. But we chose LA because it felt like a good middle meeting place, as one friend and her baby were flying to the States from Australia.

At the time I booked my cross-country flight, traveling solo with two babies didn't sound all that difficult. Maybe that's because I bought my ticket when both girls were snoozing quietly during an elongated nap. I remember looking at their peaceful, resting bodies cozied up beside me on the bed and thinking, *Awww . . . what's six hours in the air verses six hours on the ground?* I called the airline to double-check legal logistics for flying solo with two infants and purchased our tickets within a few minutes.

I bought a seat for myself and a second seat beside me for one car seat. That way, I could rotate Madalena and Beatrice, placing one into the strapped car seat while holding the other as a lap infant for nursing and playtime. In my head the game plan sounded doable, and for the most part it was. The flight to LA carried on without any major hiccups, and while finding a way to pee on the plane presented a slight challenge, the in-flight crew was like my own village thirty-six thousand feet in the sky, kindly holding my girls when my bladder was about to burst as we glided through the clouds toward California.

Our week in LA was special. My friends and I rented a house with a quiet backyard, where we mostly ordered in, held one another's babies in our arms, and talked late into the night about everything from our college days to life as we know it now, with encouraging insights and wisdom shared collectively. Our babies played, we laughed and cried, and the week ended sooner than I wanted it to.

The morning of our travel day home, I prepped myself by smearing additional layers of deodorant under my arms while getting ready. *I can do hard things*, I chanted in my head in between singing lullabies loudly, since both girls decided to scream in unison on the drive to the airport. Once at the curb, my nose detected a red alert of two fragrant diapers, and in my haste of trying to steer my bags, double stroller, car seats, and babies through the bathroom changing station, we mysteriously wound up with a broken car-seat strap once through security.

Despite wanting to crawl everywhere and touch everything, as babies do, both girls were troopers during our flight delays (minus the moment one licked a trash can, but that's more on me than her, right?). I originally had planned to delay naptime so both of them could sleep in the air, but as our takeoff time continued to suspend just out of reach, I needed to restrategize.

I hadn't gotten far before Madalena fell asleep in my arms. With superb comedic timing, the attendant behind the desk at our gate sounded off on the airport speaker: "Ladies and gentlemen, we are now inviting passengers with small children and any passengers requiring special assistance to begin boarding at this time." I looked down at Madalena, knowing that despite even my best ninja-mom moves, I'd disrupt her nap as I tried to carry her, her sister, and all of our gear onto the flight.

I can do hard things, I repeated in my head, pumping myself up for an overly tired and rightfully angry baby upon takeoff.

We boarded the flight to the last row, where I'd intentionally chosen our seats (somehow I believed we'd be less visible/annoying/obnoxious to fellow passengers by camping out in the far back corner). While tired and dazed from being abruptly awoken after a few moments of sleep, Madalena eventually fell back into a restful slumber in the car seat after nursing. I slowly broke away from her hold so I could tend to Beatrice, who patiently awaited her turn for milk and sleep, while I also tried to quietly situate our heap of supplies and bags before takeoff. As Beatrice's eyelids began to close, I shut my own and leaned into the headrest behind me. *I can do hard things*, I repeated.

It felt possible the more I said it. Each time, those words carried me a bit further toward my goal of crawling into my own bed some three thousand miles across the country—after a long day of travel, after kissing my husband and older three children whom I'd missed all week, and after tucking my two babies into their own beds. I was so close. *I can do hard things.* The image of my bed strengthened me, and the goal of falling into it helped my resolve to stay calm and carry on.

Beatrice shifted in my arms, startling me awake. And that's when I noticed both babies slowly waking up. I checked my phone for the time. It had only been forty-five minutes. Naptime was ending. I looked out the window. We weren't anywhere near the sky, or even the runway. *We were still parked at the terminal!*

Another delay, another diaper blowout, a full container of Cheerios spilled with a water bottle cap leak inside my diaper bag, plus two babies who struggled with their ears during our landing close to sunset . . . the six hours in the sky felt like thirty at times. Once at baggage claim in New York, I struggled to drag my luggage, double stroller, and car seats across the crosswalk to the taxi pickup line. I eventually paid someone twenty dollars to help me cross the street with my things, since the airport was out of the luggage carts I had hoped to rely on when planning my packing list.

It was dark and well past bedtime when our taxi cleared the

Holland Tunnel to enter New York City. I called Josh to update him on our whereabouts. "Will you meet us on the street in front of our apartment? I didn't bring my keys," I explained.

"Of course," he replied. "Text when you're a few blocks away . . ."

With both girls restless and exhausted, our taxi pulled up to the corner of our apartment building about half an hour later. I'd both texted and called Josh several times, but he didn't respond. "Do you need help getting inside?" my taxi driver asked as he unloaded the last of my things while I held both of my girls.

"Well, my husband is on his way down, so I should be okay . . ." I tried to sound confident though I wasn't sure. "Thank you anyway."

And then, at ten o'clock at night, after a travel day that began in LA at six-something in the morning, with multiple delays and fun obstacles and exciting diaper blowouts, Beatrice, Madalena, and I found ourselves sitting on our apartment stoop, locked out of our building. *He totally fell asleep*, I thought. *My husband, my knight in shining armor, is totally, completely sound asleep.* My bandwidth felt shot, and I didn't know if I could mentally or physically get us any further.

I can do hard things, I said to myself, resisting the urge to cry and break down.

I began to call neighbors in the building, while buzzing our apartment and other apartments on the door buzzer, without success. I called friends in the neighborhood, only to get their voice mails. Half an hour went by. I tried to sing to my girls on the stoop as they pointed to the door. I started to consider leaving my car seats on the stoop and loading my girls into their double stroller, with our suitcase on my back, and walking to the nearest hotel. As I picked up the girls once again, I realized I was out of diapers.

Josh called. Finally. "I'm sorry! I'm here! I fell asleep! I'm coming down!"

He opened the door to our apartment building and I couldn't even look at him. "I'm very upset," I began, using my hands to reiterate the messaging. "And we probably should not speak for a good twenty minutes."

But roasting Josh for falling asleep isn't the point of this. The point is that having an empowering phrase to repeat grounded me in a difficult day and saved me from giving up hours earlier, and even right at the finish line. Years prior, I'd learned that my children feed off my energy and my mood. I firmly believe reciting the phrase *I can do hard things* numerous times dur-

We can do hard things.

ing a day that felt impossibly hard helped me keep calm and remain in check, which, in turn, helped my two baby girls feel calm and safe and as pleasant and chill as they could be for one-year-old babies during a tricky, long day.

Even with countless moments when I wanted to throw my arms up and yell, "*Seriously?!*" (and one or two moments when I contemplated ordering my first-ever glass of wine), I knew I could handle it—just like you can handle it. Because we *can* do hard things.

At times we'll be asked to do what feels impossible. Or we won't even be asked but will be tossed straight in. Possibly daily! Into challenges much harder and deeper and rawer than a stupid, insignificant travel day with two babies. And while it's okay to throw our arms up sometimes and say, *"What the what?!"* we can also remind ourselves *I can do hard things*—and then do them. Because we can. Because we will. Because we already do.

Acknowledgments

Not to get all sobby on you, but my eyes feel a little fuzzy as I attempt to blink back the tears just thinking of all the good people who have helped me bring this book to life. As I start to write these acknowledgments, I am roughly thirty seconds away from an ugly cry of happy tears.

I have to begin with you, my blog readers and social media friends. Thank you to those who have followed along since my early blogging years. (Some of you have been with me since way back in the olden days of 2007!) Thank you for reading my blog posts, commenting, emailing, and lending support and love way back then and in the years that have followed. Thank you to those who have joined the party since (it's a party, right?!), be it years ago or a few months back, or even just yesterday. Thank you for following along on different social channels and building such a strong community in the online space where we've been able to grow and learn and share together. Thank you for using my neighborhood and travel guides, for pinning my photos, and for remaining with me even during that long period of time where I couldn't quite quit the Nashville filter on Insta. Thank you for praying for my family. I have felt your prayers, and countless times over the years, I have leaned on them.

I want to thank God. For giving each of us unique gifts to

build on and for giving each of us a direct line of communication with Him, through prayer and personal revelation. I'll say some variation of it until I am blue in the face (am I blue yet?!), but navigating life's twists and turns and maddening-volume-level-of-noise is never easy. However, leaning on Him while tuning in to my own inner compass is something I'm forever thankful for.

Thank you to my literary agents, Celeste Fine and Anna Petkovich, and also the Park & Fine team, for their warmth and excitement surrounding this project.

Celeste, who would have thought that when we officially met in the summer of 2018, at a café around the corner from my apartment to discuss this possible book, we'd piece together a random first interaction just a few months prior that felt fortuitous then and even now? When, at thirty-six weeks pregnant with my twin girls, I'd waddled onto the 1 train on the west side of Manhattan, and you, another train passenger, would share a kind interaction and few words of encouragement with me, a then stranger. Thank you for your wisdom and discernment in each interaction since that first brief brush on the subway. I am so grateful to have your intelligence and guidance in this process.

And Anna, thank you for reading my blog from the beginning. Thank you for believing in me and my writing. Thank you for your encouragement as I have asked all the silly questions along the way. Thank you for the soft yet firm reminders to trust myself in this process. And thank you for your patience as we put a timeline into play, and then I paused everything and sat on this for a very long time, realizing I needed to first get my bearings with my baby girls, as our family navigated becoming a little bit bigger and a little bit messier with our two newest additions.

Thank you to HarperCollins and, more specifically, everyone

at Harper Horizon who has given such support and love from the beginning.

Thank you to my publisher, Andrea Fleck-Nisbet. In our very first meeting, you shared that your goal for your new imprint was to be deliberate in acquiring authors and books focused on sharing messages from the heart, on being kind. That spoke to me then and now, and I thank you for putting your imprint's focus on a direction that has the potential to help change the world. Thank you for trusting my voice and giving me the chance to accomplish my goal of writing my book entirely on my own, without the support of a coauthor or ghostwriter.

Thank you to my editor, Amanda Bauch, for putting up with all my run-on sentences and challenging me as a writer as I tackled proper grammar and punctuation for, like, the first time ever. Amanda, I love learning from you—from your emails on all things book related to so many things outside of this project, as you generously shared insights and takeaways with me on many other areas of life. During this writing process, I greatly appreciated your coaxing to stay true to my own style of writing (even as I chose to keep a lot of those run-on sentences in the book) and maybe used the word *stet* wrong during copyedits. Get fancy, yeah?

Thank you to Julie Cantrell, who, from an accomplished writer's perspective, gave me critical tools and helpful tips to analyze my writing, as the Park & Fine team and I began the book-proposal process. This early writing lesson was so very valuable, Julie, but I often think about your heartfelt wisdom and cheers as I started hearing some noise and doubts delving into this process solo. I still remember our conversations on the phone, when you offered kind words of encouragement, giving me a boost in confidence to know that my story mattered, that my writing was good, and that my voice was going to make a difference and help even just one woman out there. Thank you, thank you.

Thank you to the village of women in my life who have shaped so much of who I am today, through our shared seasons. Thank you to my girlfriends who mother hard, love fiercely, and always have time for my rambling video messages at three in the morning, covering all the important things in life—like Taylor Swift's latest album to a play-by-play of me cooking my first chicken casserole for my children that my children never even ate.

Thank you to my parents for the support you have shown over the years as I've carved my own path. Thank you for making us laugh again and again, Dad, by having five dozen jokes and puns and stories up your sleeve at any given moment. And thank you, Mom, for passing on family heritage and traditions, like the delicious homemade pierogi I love so much. Most importantly, thank you both for your blessing to share parts of my story in this book that we experienced together.

Thank you to Hannah, Rachel, and Rebekah, my three intelligent, beautiful, and good-hearted sisters. I might be the eldest, but I look up to each of you and your caring examples in countless ways. Thank you for giving me a safe space in our frequent conversations and calls and interactions always, but during this writing process specifically. I am so proud of the women you are and the light you give.

A very big thank-you to my husband, Josh. This book, just like so many other things in my life, would have remained a "someday dream" if it weren't for you. Thank you for sorting out so many parts of this project as I focused on the writing. Thank you for the countless times you loaded all five kids up and out the door, so I could type with both hands instead of only one. Thank you for being my best friend, my hype-man, my biggest supporter. Thank you for loving me on my good days and my bad days and during all the hair changes too. Thank you for repeatedly double-spacing each chapter of the manuscript, as I'd repeatedly forget how to do it. And thank you for never acting annoyed as you patiently walked me through each step of the double-spacing process once again. You are what good stuff is made of, and I am the luckiest to have you by my side.

Thank you to my children—Eleanor, Samson, Conrad, Madalena, and Beatrice. Eleanor, you happily (and very well, might I add) proofread some chapters for me, and Samson, you asked many inquisitive questions about the book-writing process while also once commenting that maybe my book would fall in the *comedy* genre you so dearly love, stating that some of my sentences were funny. (Thank you, Samson.) Conrad, as I worked on chapters, you cuddled beside me and sounded out several words as they appeared on my screen. No one can spot the letter C as fast as you. Madalena and Beatrice, you greeted me excitedly as I reemerged from hiding in my closet or locked bathroom or back bedroom, trying to finish this book, and you gave me the biggest hugs while asking about my "buuuuhh!" I want all five of you to know how much I love you and thank you for your patience with Mama as I've felt a deliberate pull and urgency to share this message with the world, *now*.

Eleanor, Samson, Conrad, Beatrice, and Madalena, as you grow and move through the noise of life, if anything, may these words from your mama be a gentle nudge to trust and love yourselves, so you can confidently embrace your own beautiful adventures. Thank you for bringing so much joy into my world. You're my five reasons why, and I love each of you very much.

About the Author

Naomi Davis, named a Forbes Top Ten Parenting Influencer, shares happy and helpful stories across her social media channels and award-winning website. What started in 2007 as an online journal about her newlywed life in New York City while a Juilliard dance student, *Love Taza* has amassed a loyal following, reaching millions around the world. Now, Naomi continues to inspire audiences with vibrant photos, engaging videos, and heartfelt words that document her adventures parenting five young children, traveling near and far, celebrating life's simple joys, and finding purpose in the everyday.

As @taza, Naomi has created and produced dozens of successful branded campaigns for top companies large and small. Fun accomplishments include launching a limited-edition family travel collection at Target stores nationwide and being invited to the White House by Michelle Obama to discuss the former first lady's Let's Move! initiative. Alongside her husband, Josh, Naomi lives in a sort-of-always-messy home with five little cookie monsters who like to sing, dance, read, tell jokes, make toast, or do anything else to delay their bedtimes.